Reclaiming the *Heart* of Marriage

David A. Shadday

Eight-Session Bible Study

CONCORDIA PUBLISHING HOUSE · SAINT LOUIS

Published by Concordia Publishing House
3558 S. Jefferson Ave., St. Louis, MO 63118–3968
1-800-325-3040 • cph.org

Manufactured in the United States of America

1 2 3 4 5 6 7 8 9 10 33 32 31 30 29 28 27 26 25 24

Contents

Introduction 5

Tips for Leaders and Participants 9

LESSON 1 The Covenant of Salvation 11

LESSON 2 Definitions 19

LESSON 3 The Old Testament Marriage Covenant Affirmed 33

LESSON 4 God's Response to Israel's Sinfulness 45

LESSON 5 The Song of Solomon: The Ephesians 5 of the Old Testament 55

LESSON 6 Marriage Covenant Language in the Gospels 65

LESSON 7 Marriage Covenant Language in the Epistles and Revelation 75

LESSON 8 Ephesians 5: The Song of Solomon of the New Testament 85

Leader Guide

LESSON 1 The Covenant of Salvation 93

LESSON 2 Definitions 101

LESSON 3 The Old Testament Marriage Covenant Affirmed 107

LESSON 4 God's Response to Israel's Sinfulness 113

LESSON 5 The Song of Solomon: The Ephesians 5 of the Old Testament 119

LESSON 6 Marriage Covenant Language in the Gospels 129

LESSON 7 Marriage Covenant Language in the Epistles and Revelation 135

LESSON 8 Ephesians 5: The Song of Solomon of the New Testament 141

APPENDIX Ancient Jewish Weddings 145

INTRODUCTION

REALITY AND REFLECTION

Like so many things that change our lives, this Bible study started in a simple way: a simple question to a pastor at a youth meeting. A young lady wanted to know why there was such a thing as marriage. Clearly, God commanded it. But why? The pastor obviously knew that marriage is instituted by God, but he paused to ask himself why. Then he told the young lady he would look at Scripture and give her an answer after careful study and thought. He studied this topic for the rest of his life, and he shared his thoughts with people along the way.

Among those with whom he shared those thoughts were the couples who came to him for premarital counseling. The soon-to-be groom of one of those couples was a young man about to begin his seminary training. He was fascinated with the application of Christ and the church that the pastor made in their sessions together. After sitting at the pastor's feet, the young student began to search the Scriptures for a greater understanding of what he had learned. I was that young man. My journey in searching Scripture has been a wondrous one, giving greater clarity to humanity's relationship with God and the realization of the incredible expression of faith found in what God instituted in the Garden of Eden. It is my prayer that you will join me on that journey.

Before we proceed, it is necessary to discuss biblical imagery. The Bible speaks in image terminology. Some of this language is about certain people ("Judah is a lion's cub," Genesis 49:9) or, in many references, God's people. Much of this language is used for God. Some of the language about God is spoken in literal terms, such as the following: "The LORD is my shepherd" (Psalm 23:1); "The God of Jacob is our fortress" (Psalm 46:7); and "The LORD is my rock" (Psalm 18:2). While these are biblical images, the language is powerful. What is clearly biblical imagery is spoken of in very literal terms, as the above references show. Our relationship to God is so powerfully described in this imagery that we speak of Him—and His relationship to us—in similar or identical terms in our hymns and liturgy.

Within the following lessons, you will look at marriage as a reflection of the relationship between Jesus and His Bride, the church. A husband and wife are to reflect their marital relationship in the same pattern as Jesus and the church. This will be a new viewpoint for most of you. Normally, we view relationships between men and women as the relationships we should reflect instead of the relationship between Christ and the church. In this discussion, you will see yourselves as reflecting a greater reality—the marriage covenant of salvation between Christ and the church.

What are you reflecting in this relationship? You are not to reflect what God demands in His Law but what He has done for you in Christ Jesus. You will see how relationships confess what we believe about our faith. You will discuss the meaning of the relationship between Christ and His church as you live in love within the marriage relationship God has established for your spouse and you.

The principles discussed in this study are the timeless truths expressed in God's Word. They are substantially different from constantly changing social fads and philosophies. God's Word calls you to see the wonders He has prepared for you in the light of the grace He has given you in Christ. Throughout this study, you will hear God's call to love as you have been loved by Jesus, even though you live in a world dominated by expectations and obligations (Law). You will see how your basic relationships are defined and motivated by the Good News of Jesus' death and resurrection, foretold in the Old Testament and fulfilled in the New Testament.

Each day, you participate in habits and behaviors simply because they've been passed down from generation to generation (like when men open doors for women). You just do them, even if you aren't internally motivated by doing good. The reasons for such behaviors range from "I told you so" to "That's how you should act." Through this study, you will discuss how your lives as a husband and wife reflect the relationship you have with God. Your examples and motivations are not based on what God expects you to do but on the loving relationship Christ has with us, His Bride, the church.

The applications discussed in this Bible study may seem idealistic or theoretical to many who consider them for the first time. They are neither idealistic nor theoretical for my wife nor me. We have sought to apply them to our life together—imperfectly because we are sinners but in a way that has been an unspeakable blessing to our marriage because God the Holy Spirit has blessed us not simply in understanding this idea but in the daily grace to love each other in the love of Christ. You will also begin a journey that most have never intentionally been on. It is a journey to understand the love God has for you, your response to His love, and the meaning that love brings into your life and your home.

TIPS FOR LEADERS AND PARTICIPANTS

- Listen to the biblical text. Much of what you will hear in this study will likely be new to you. If you have never read many of these texts, they will require you to consider some things you have not previously thought about. Be convinced by the biblical text itself. Draw your conclusions, even if they disagree with one another, from what the Bible says.
- Consider carefully what you want to share in discussions with other participants. If there are things about your life that you consider personal, do not feel any obligation to share them.
- Some participants may share personal things, especially if these are small group discussions. Don't automatically assume that something shared in that context should be shared with others.
- Don't be afraid to ask questions. Contemplating questions that had not been previously asked is how this study came to be in the first place. The answers to your questions may be simple, complex, or unknown. Some of the unknown answers may be unknowable. Others may open a new line of inquiry on a relatively new topic in the twenty-first century.
- If this study causes you to change how you live, let those changes be slow, calm, and a response to God's calling to you in Christ. I have no interest in the marriage covenant of salvation being a fad, but I hope it is a blessing to you, just as it has been a blessing to my wife and me.

THE COVENANT OF SALVATION

GOD'S REALITY

JEREMIAH 31:33–34

33For this is the covenant that I will make with the house
of Israel after those days, declares the Lord: I will put
My law within them, and I will write it on their hearts.
And I will be their God, and they shall be My people.
34And no longer shall each one teach his neighbor and
each his brother, saying, "Know the Lord," for they shall
all know Me, from the least of them to the greatest, declares the Lord. For I will forgive their iniquity, and I
will remember their sin no more.

WHAT IS A COVENANT?

There is so much talk in Christian circles these days about covenants and covenant relationships. Understanding what people are talking about when it comes to covenants is sometimes difficult.

Many people understand a covenant to be a kind of contract between two basically equal and consenting parties. Others define a covenant as a promise to be fulfilled by some action in the future.

What does God mean by the word *covenant*? This is the vital issue. We are not free to impose our views of the word *covenant* on God and His Word. Our task is to determine what God means when He makes a covenant with His people. To understand the approach this study takes on marriage, one must understand what a covenant is in God's Word.

Is our covenant relationship to God a promise to be fulfilled in the future? Not primarily. God certainly promised to send the Messiah, who fulfilled His covenant with Israel. That took place in Jesus' death and resurrection. Since Christ has come, fulfilling His mission, ours is not primarily a covenant of promise but of promise fulfilled. Is our covenant with God a contract between two basically equal and consenting parties? Clearly not!

OLD TESTAMENT COVENANTS BETWEEN GOD AND HIS PEOPLE

In the Old Testament, God made various covenants with His people, all pointing to fulfillment in the Messiah, who saved us. Read the passages listed below in your Bibles and consider what they show you about covenants in the Old Testament.

- Read about the covenant of circumcision in Genesis 17:1–14.
- Read about the Passover covenant in Exodus 13:3–16.
- Read about the covenant made on the Day of Atonement in Leviticus 16.

God made other covenants with Israel, but these help us understand the kind of covenant discussed in this study.

THE MARRIAGE COVENANT OF SALVATION

The covenant between God and His people is the covenant of salvation. Jesus came into the world to bear our sins on the cross. He rose from the dead to confirm His promises to us and has ascended to the throne of heaven as the Lamb who was slain to confirm the covenant before the Father for all time. God sends His Holy Spirit to create and sustain faith in us. That faith receives His loving sacrifice for us and clings to it in all circumstances. In this covenant, God does everything to make us His own.

This relationship is described in Scripture as the marriage covenant of salvation. The teaching of the marriage covenant of salvation is described in image language in the Old and New Testament texts that we will discuss in upcoming lessons. As we will see, these texts vary when it comes to describing a certain aspect of God's covenant relationship, but they all have imagery that defines and reflects a marriage relationship. Like some other image language, such as Psalm 23:1, "The Lord is my Shepherd," the marriage image language often employs rather literal language (e.g., Isaiah 54:5, "Your Maker is your husband). God uses this marriage imagery language to describe the covenant of salvation. He next applies the Old Testament relationship He has described to Christ and the church in Ephesians 5:22–33. Then He uses Christ and the church to teach a husband and wife the pattern they are to follow in their marriage. Thus, the actual marriage relationship between a Christian couple is defined by the image of the marriage covenant of salvation between God and His people.

In the marriage covenant of salvation, God gives us everything, and we receive it. He gives us His Word of Law and Gospel. The Law shows us our sin and drives us from our works to the need for forgiveness. The Gospel assures us of forgiveness and eternal salvation through the death and resurrection of Christ. The Law and Gospel do the same for a married couple. The Law shows the couple their sins against God and each other, while the Gospel offers and gives forgiveness and motivates that couple to forgive as they have been forgiven.

Jesus is the center of God's covenant with us. He is the Savior. We focus on the cross because Christ crucified our sins there, removing the barrier between God and us. Jesus made us children of God by His death and resurrection. To be centered on Christ is to be centered on what He did for us in His death and resurrection. Our life is found in Christ and Christ alone. What He did for us makes us Christians and serves as both our motivation and example as we live our lives. In this Bible study, you will investigate how the marriage covenant of salvation is the relationship that defines marriage and how it has become the pattern for Christian men and women who are married.

In the Old Testament, we see salvation portrayed as a marriage covenant. That marriage covenant is fulfilled in Jesus and His relationship to His Bride, the church. This study will discuss both Old and New Testament references to the marriage covenant and will show how God's covenant with us defines and informs Christian marriage. This focus is on Christ promised and Christ fulfilled—the basis for the covenant we have with God.

REFLECTIONS ON GOD AND HIS PEOPLE

1. What kind of covenant has God made with us? How does this differ from covenants, commitments, and contracts we make in the world?

2. How does the covenant God made with us differ from covenants we have made with others?

3. What is God's covenant based on? What does this mean in our relationship to Him?

4. **Based on our understanding of God's covenant with us, what does it mean to center our lives on Christ?**

____

____

____

____

5. **Similarly, what does it mean to center our relationships on Christ?**

____

____

____

____

6. **Most importantly for this conversation, what does it mean to center marriage on Christ?**

____

____

____

____

7. **What is different about your view of covenant relationships after reading through this lesson?**

____

____

____

____

8. **What do you hope to find in the following lessons to help you understand how our covenant relationship with God affects our relationships?**

____

____

____

____

DEFINITIONS

"What does this mean?" These are familiar words for many from Luther's Small Catechism. This lesson will examine what God means by some key terms that help us understand our relationship with Him and our relationships with one another.

GOD'S REALITY

To understand the application of the marriage covenant of salvation and how we reflect Christ and the church, we must first define certain terms. Competing definitions in society prevent us from assuming that we all mean the same thing when we speak of love or authority. We will define these terms as they are defined in Scripture so we can come to an understanding of what God means when He uses them. This will clear the way for us to apply these concepts, by faith, to our lives.

LOVE DEFINED

The first term we must clearly define is *love*. The word *love* can mean a whole host of things, many of which have little to do with one another and nothing to do with the biblical definition. When I say, "I love my wife," it cannot mean the same thing as when I say, "I love pizza." Yet the same English word is employed in both sentences.

One of the many uses of the term *love* in speech is the phrase "Making love." This is a reference to sexual intercourse. Present American society is obsessed with sexual intercourse. Because of this, the term *love* has been hijacked by free-sex advocates. At the same time, infatuation with someone is often called "love." This infatuation requires no substance to qualify it as such. Likewise, lust is called "love." In this context, many refer to acting on that lust (totally devoid of any substantive relationship) as "making love." This "love" is nothing more than the satisfaction of animal pleasures without thinking about commitment or consequences. It is simply acting upon infatuation or lust to release a sexual urge. None of these examples exemplify love. Infatuation could become love if that infatuation leads one to get to know and grow in love with another person of the opposite sex. Lust could conceivably lead to love if a relationship that grows into something of substance is established. Though it's unlikely that infatuation will lead to love, it is possible. But in and of themselves, neither infatuation nor love bear any resemblance to biblical love. Surrendering yourself to love as the world defines it is imprisoning yourself in a shallow, baseless relationship that will crumble at the first sign of trouble because it is built on nothing of substance. God has called us to much more.

Love in our sinful world is also defined by a sense of kinship with others. This is experienced in some families as a kind of regard, like between siblings or other extended family members. Although kindred relationships can be strong, they are not as strong as the love described by God in the Bible. One can have love for his or her community, country, or even special objects. That is not the kind of love God is referring to when He calls us to love.

All of these examples, as well as the other popular definitions of "love," focus on emotion. Modern society sees love as primarily, or entirely, an emotion. Truly, love includes emotion, but is it primarily an emotion? Or does love have a substance that produces emotion and makes it part of the whole instead of the focus? Is love what I feel, or is what I feel produced by and a part of love? We live in an emotion-driven society. Scripture, however, teaches that love is not primarily an emotion. An emotional response to loved ones is produced in us by the substance of true love.

God defines what love is. We might feel God's love, but that feeling does not confirm that God loves us. That confirmation is instead found in the substance of God's action through His Son on the cross. Do we know God loves us because we feel it? Not really. We know God loves us because He showed us He does. "God so loved the world, that He gave His only Son, that whoever believes in Him should not perish but have eternal life" (John 3:16). We know love because we have been loved by God. That love is plainly before us on the cross, where Jesus loved us by taking away our sins. This is the only definition of love we will ever need. We have been loved by Jesus, filled with that love by the Holy Spirit, and empowered by the Holy Spirit to show it to others. The apostle John makes this point in 1 John 4:10–11: "In this is love, not that we have loved God but that He loved us and sent His Son to be the propitiation for our sins. Beloved, if God so loved us, we also ought to love one another." Are you looking for love? Go to the cross! What Jesus did for us on the cross—that's love!

Our challenge is not to define love. God has defined love for us. Having received that love, we are called to show it to others and thank God for having received it in the first place. Showing the love of Christ has nothing to do with what is expected of us. Love is our expression of thanks, in faith, for the love God has shown us in Christ.

How do we show that love? Many would answer that question with the words of Scripture: "Love your neighbor as yourself" (Leviticus 19:18; Matthew 19:19). To make this the defining Scripture on love is to mistake the minimum expectations of the Law for the love found only in God. To love others as we love ourselves is the basic expectation of God's Law, but we don't even do that. Jesus points us to a higher calling in love when He says in John 15:12–13, "Love one another as I have loved you. Greater love has no one than this, that someone lay down his life for his friends." This love is only possible by receiving the love Jesus has shown us on the cross and responding to it by showing that same love to others. This is the work of the Holy Spirit in us by faith.

What can we learn from the cross about love? First, we can learn that love is not the mere satisfaction of an expectation (God's or ours). If one loves according to expectation, then when the expectation is met, one is free to stop loving. Jesus never stops loving us. In His love for us, He surpasses the expectations of the Law without even acknowledging that they are there. As He journeyed to the cross, Jesus was not driven by the expectations of the Father—or our expectations. Jesus' love compelled Him to go to the cross and give Himself totally. Thus, Jesus defines love as being a complete giving of oneself without regard for the expectations of others or one's needs. It is the total willingness to sacrifice something for the one you love.

Second, love is centered on others. Society too often wants us to do things because of "what's in it for me." Sinful humanity is self-centered. We are motivated by selfishness to do everything from buying a particular product to community service. Too often, we are motivated to do some worthwhile activity so we can feel better about ourselves. This is not the way with Jesus. Jesus died for our sins because He loves us. Love brought Him to completely pour Himself out, even unto death. Jesus held nothing back in loving us. This is essential to the love He shows us and gives us to show others. To love someone is to give of yourself totally for that loved one—without regard for whether that love is returned. This is the love Jesus has for us.

This love is a privilege, not an obligation. We don't love because we have to or because we should. We love because we have the privilege to show the love of Jesus to people in our lives. What a privilege it is to have the love of Jesus! He has blessed us with the wonders of His grace. As we communicate with people in our lives, we have a rich and special privilege to show them Jesus by our love. Each day, we encounter many people to whom we should show the love of Jesus. Expectations cause us to ask, "Do I have to?" Love causes us to say, "I have the privilege to show the love of Jesus to this person for whom Christ died." Jesus has treasured us in love. By giving us His love, He empowers us to see all people as precious children for whom He died. Since they are precious to Him, they are also precious to us. Treasure those God has given us by loving them as you have been loved by Christ.

1. **What different definitions of love do you encounter? What's wrong with the false ones? How do those definitions fall short of truly fulfilling people's lives?**

2. **Where do we go to find a true definition of the word *love*? Why? What does it mean that God is love? What does that have to do with the cross?**

3. **What is the role of self-sacrifice in love? How do we know that? How can you show the self-sacrificial love of Jesus to people in your life? Be specific.**

4. Why should you show love to others? Where is that love centered (on others or yourself)? Whom has God given you to love? How can you center your love on them? Be specific.

____

____

____

____

5. Is love an obligation or a privilege? What does that mean when you show it? How does it affect your attitude? Whom has God given you the privilege to love? How do you desire to show those people Christ? Be specific.

____

____

____

____

AUTHORITY AS SERVICE

It is fitting, at this point, to affirm the biblical definition of the word *authority* so we can dispel all false assumptions. The world views authority in various ways. In most cases, it is the exercise of power of one sort or another. Along with this power comes, in many instances, domination. For example, for many, a boss's power includes the ability to dictate the actions of others. In marriage, this perception of authority is exemplified in the male domination of women, especially when a man takes improper advantage of his wife's caring and serving nature. The exercise of authority in the home is, unfortunately, too often caricatured as a picture of a man flexing his muscles with one foot on his wife's back as she scrubs the floor. Holding to this view too often leads to abuse and the dehumanization of married women. This definition of authority in marriage is what the feminist movement originally objected to, and rightly so, in the 1800s.

Authority in the world also includes privilege. In society, this is demonstrated by the perks of one's position. In the home, this is demonstrated by the delegation of responsibilities with no regard to primary accountability or leadership in fulfilling them. Many see this as the privilege a man has to hand his wife a list of jobs for her to do as he heads out the door with his golf clubs over his shoulder. We see this attitude cruelly taken to its logical conclusion in the virtual enslavement of many married women in their homes. The world's view of authority leads to cruel dictatorship under the law of the head.

This view of authority, however, bears no resemblance whatsoever to Jesus Christ and the exercise of His authority. His authority is total and absolute (Matthew 28:18). But the exercise and meaning of that authority is entirely different from dictatorship. Three texts in Scripture demonstrate the Christian concept of authority.

In Mark 9:33–37, the disciples wondered which of them would be the greatest in the kingdom of God. They knew they were specially chosen by Christ and argued about their place on the totem pole of God's kingdom. No doubt this conversation included a discussion of the merits of each for such a place. What each considered his pedigree to be is unknown, but they no doubt had reasons for why they thought they were worthy of esteem in the eyes of our

Lord. Jesus then defined greatness in a way that no doubt humbled them and ended the discussion. He pointed out that whoever wishes to be great must be the servant of the rest.

Jesus made the same point in Matthew 20:20–28. The mother of the sons of Zebedee requested that her sons sit at Jesus' right hand and left hand in His kingdom. This request caused a disturbance among the disciples. Jesus pointed out that although the rulers of the world exercise absolute authority (domination, dictatorship), it would not be so among the disciples. He then repeated the assertion that the greatest is the servant or slave of the rest. He concluded by using Himself as an example. He who has all authority in heaven and on earth points out that "the Son of Man came not to be served but to serve, and to give His life as a ransom for many" (v. 28). Jesus pointed them away from any pedigree of who they were to loving service, using His sacrifice on the cross as the ultimate example of that service.

The third text that clearly makes this point is the account of Jesus washing the disciples' feet in John 13:1–20. Here, Jesus stripped to the waist to do the work of a slave. When He got to Peter, He was refused. Peter could not allow Jesus to humiliate Himself with the work of a slave. Jesus then made the remarkable statement that if He did not wash Peter's feet, Peter would have no part in Him. Jesus' words seem awfully harsh until they are closely examined. If Peter would not let Jesus serve him in a small matter, how would he ever submit to Jesus' saving service on the cross? Peter relented, and the process was completed. Jesus then pointed out that to be a leader in His kingdom means performing such service to those entrusted to one's care. He defined the exercise of authority as service. This is in direct contrast to authority as exercised in the world. Jesus turned one's perception of the exercise of authority on its head by defining the one in authority as the greatest servant.

In the image of the marriage covenant of salvation, the relationship between Christ and His church, we see this truth clearly expressed. Christ's headship is expressed in the words "as Christ loved the church and gave Himself up for her, that He might sanctify her, having cleansed her by the washing of water with the word, so that He might present the church to Himself in splendor, without spot or wrinkle or any such thing, that she might be holy and without blemish" (Ephesians 5:25–27). All of these things are for her benefit, not His. Jesus' authority is expressed in how He magnifies the church by His loving service, particularly in His death on the cross for her. How is His exercise of authority judged? It is judged by how greatly He served His Bride. This is the standard He establishes not only by His words but by His actions on our behalf. Jesus never served Himself. By tempting Jesus in the wilderness, Satan intended to get Jesus to serve Himself instead of us. Jesus prevailed against those and all of Satan's attempts to distract Him from His purpose: to serve us with His ultimate sacrifice. Thus, the cross is the definition of how to exercise authority. By this definition, the president should be the greatest servant in his or her country, and the boss should be the greatest servant in his or her business. The application of Ephesians 5 makes the husband the greatest servant in the home. This is a high standard. Even though sinful men cannot be exactly like Christ, they still need to view Him as the model to joyfully follow. We reflect the Gospel in the shadow of the cross, first as our source of forgiveness, and then as our motivation.

In this definition, we see Christ as the Head of the marriage relationship taking full accountability for His Bride. Headship means ultimate accountability. Adam, as head, bears the accountability for original sin (Genesis 3; Romans 5; 1 Corinthians 15). Christ voluntarily takes on the full accountability Himself for what His Bride, by right, possesses. This is the essence of His action in establishing the marriage covenant. He takes what is hers and bears it in her stead.

Jesus completely changes the definition of authority. The world sees authority as the ability to be the boss. Christians, following the definition of Christ, view authority as the ability to lead by loving service. The world sees authority as forcefully making others accomplish one's will. Jesus accomplishes His will by His self-sacrificial service for us in His death and resurrection. Jesus is the biblical definition of authority. The exercise of authority for Christians reflects the self-sacrificial love Jesus has shown us. This is a response of thanks for what we have received from Him. Jesus leads us by loving us. We are called to lead by loving others. When a woman is involved in a car accident, she does not need her husband to yell and scream at her for what she is already heartsick about. She needs love, forgiveness, and help in dealing with the circumstances. Her husband can step in with the love of Christ and fill the gap she feels, providing stability and loving care. We show our thanks and love for Jesus by showing His love to those He has placed in our care. In the light of the cross and empty tomb, the Bible defines authority as service.

REFLECTIONS ON GOD AND HIS PEOPLE

6. **What is the world's view of authority? How is it flawed? What examples of bad use of authority in the workplace can you give? What examples can you give of bad use of authority in society or in government?**

7. **What abuse of authority takes place in the home? What is wrong with these examples of people abusing their authority? What attitudes lead to such abuse of authority? What happens to lives and relationships with this flawed definition of authority in the home?**

8. How did Jesus define authority in Mark 9:33–37? How did He enhance this point in Matthew 20:20–28? What did He teach His disciples in John 13:1–20?

____

____

____

____

9. What authority does Jesus have? See Matthew 28:18. How does He exercise that authority? How does Jesus' death and resurrection define authority?

____

____

____

____

10. Why should we adopt the definition of authority used in this lesson? How does it express our faith? How can a Christian boss confess his or her faith through his or her business? How can people in authority lead those in their care to greater achievement?

____

____

____

____

11. What is authority? How does this definition of authority call you to change? How can you confess your faith in the way you exercise your authority? How will this definition of authority change lives and relationships?

____

____

____

____

THE OLD TESTAMENT MARRIAGE COVENANT AFFIRMED

Have you read these words from Psalm 45 before? This lesson introduces you to a wondrous Old Testament teaching. The focus is on God's grace to His people, including His promised grace when He sends Jesus to save His people from their sins.

GOD'S REALITY

PSALM 45

1My heart overflows with a pleasing theme;
I address my verses to the king;
my tongue is like the pen of a ready scribe.

2You are the most handsome of the sons of men;
grace is poured upon Your lips;
therefore God has blessed You forever.

3Gird Your sword on Your thigh, O mighty one,
in Your splendor and majesty!

[4]In Your majesty ride out victoriously
for the cause of truth and meekness and righteousness;
let Your right hand teach You awesome deeds!

[5]Your arrows are sharp
in the heart of the king's enemies;
the peoples fall under You.

[6]Your throne, O God, is forever and ever.
The scepter of Your kingdom is a scepter of uprightness;
[7]You have loved righteousness and hated wickedness.

Therefore God, Your God, has anointed You
with the oil of gladness beyond Your companions;
[8]Your robes are all fragrant with myrrh and aloes and cassia.

From ivory palaces stringed instruments make You glad;
[9]daughters of kings are among Your ladies of honor;
at Your right hand stands the queen in gold of Ophir.

[10]Hear, O daughter, and consider, and incline your ear:
forget your people and your father's house,
[11]and the king will desire your beauty.

Since He is your lord, bow to Him.
[12]The people of Tyre will seek your favor with gifts,
the richest of the people.

[13]All glorious is the princess in her chamber, with robes interwoven with gold.
[14]In many-colored robes she is led to the king,
with her virgin companions following behind her.

15 With joy and gladness they are led along
as they enter the palace of the king.
16 In place of Your fathers shall be Your sons;
You will make them princes in all the earth.
17 I will cause Your name to be remembered in all generations;
therefore nations will praise You forever and ever.

The first issue regarding this text is whether this is about the king of Israel or the Messiah. Many modern commentaries side with the view that this text is referring to the king of Israel. If that is so, then it lends very little to this discussion. If it refers to God (Yahweh), it is about the marriage covenant of salvation. The principal argument that Psalm 45 refers to God is the seamless manner in which addressing the king in verses 1–5 turns to addressing God in verse 6 and the remainder of the psalm.

What does this psalm contribute to the discussion of the marriage covenant of salvation? If this is a song to the heavenly Bridegroom, it affirms the Messiah, the King, as the Bridegroom. The psalm then promises joy and peace to the Bride. Who is the Bride? The context of the rest of Scripture points to Israel (the church). The focus of this text is the joy that the Bride has in the glory of the Bridegroom. This psalm affirms that the Messiah (God) is the one who brings joy to His Bride. Israel, who goes through much travail, finds her joy, hope, and offspring in the messianic Bridegroom. Verse 10 calls the Bride to forsake her own people and her father's house to cling to the King. The King desires her beauty, and she worships Him (v. 11). The King raises and glorifies her. She responds with praise and love.

1. Why does it matter whether God is the King in this psalm?

____

____

____

____

2. What is taking place in this psalm?

____

____

____

____

READ ISAIAH 54:4–8

Like the psalmist in Psalm 45, Isaiah affirms this marriage covenant in various parts of his prophecy. The first we will consider is Isaiah 54:4–8:

> [4]"Fear not, for you will not be ashamed;
> be not confounded, for you will not be disgraced;
> for you will forget the shame of your youth,
> and the reproach of your widowhood you will remember no more.
>
> [5]For your Maker is your husband,
> the LORD of hosts is His name;
> and the Holy One of Israel is your Redeemer,
> the God of the whole earth He is called.

6For the LORD has called you
like a wife deserted and grieved in spirit,
like a wife of youth when she is cast off,
says your God.

7For a brief moment I deserted you,
but with great compassion I will gather you.

8In overflowing anger for a moment
I hid My face from you,
but with everlasting love I will have compassion on you,"
says the LORD, your Redeemer.

This joyful text follows Isaiah 53—the announcement of God's grace to pay the price for our sins by the Suffering Servant. The forceful Law presentation in so much of Isaiah gives way to rejoicing in the fulfillment of the messianic covenant. It's in the context of rejoicing that this marriage covenant discussion takes place.

The heart of this text is found in verse 5 and the following verses, where, in this image, we see God identify Himself as the husband. He affirms that Israel's Maker is her husband. Then He adds that He is also the Redeemer. In the verses that follow, He affirms that, although she is forsaken for a moment, she will be redeemed and restored. God ties this marriage covenant to the concept of redemption.

3. What is the context of Isaiah 53?

___

___

___

4. Who is the husband in this text?

---

5. How does God's restoration take place? (See Isaiah 53.)

READ ISAIAH 61:8–11

Isaiah 61:8–11 attests the marriage covenant of salvation.

8For I the LORD love justice;
 I hate robbery and wrong;
I will faithfully give them their recompense,
 and I will make an everlasting covenant with them.

9Their offspring shall be known among the nations,
 and their descendants in the midst of the peoples;
all who see them shall acknowledge them,
 that they are an offspring the LORD has blessed.

10I will greatly rejoice in the LORD;
 my soul shall exult in my God,
for He has clothed me with the garments of salvation;

He has covered me with the robe of righteousness,
as a bridegroom decks himself like a priest with a beautiful
headdress,
and as a bride adorns herself with her jewels.

11 For as the earth brings forth its sprouts,
and as a garden causes what is sown in it to sprout up,
so the Lord God will cause righteousness and praise
to sprout up before all the nations.

God promises His people an everlasting covenant and an everlasting posterity. Based on God's promise, Israel responds in verses 10–11. Here we see God promising the covenant of grace and Israel (the church) responding in joy. In that response, the prophet introduces a very common theme in the texts dealing with the marriage covenant of salvation: "He has clothed me with the garments of salvation; He has covered me with the robe of righteousness" (v. 10). God dresses His Bride for the occasion of her messianic covenant relationship: the garments of salvation and righteousness.

How do the phrases in this verse relate to one another? Are they expressions layered on top of one another, or are the garments of salvation explained by the ornaments of the bridegroom and the robe of righteousness explained by the jewels? To answer this, we must first remember that salvation is what God does and is expressed by the ministry of the priests, who performed the sacrifices. Righteousness, on the other hand, is what is received as a result of that salvation. Likewise, the jewels the bride received are an expression of the groom's love for her. This relationship between the bride and bridegroom serves as an illustration of God's action and Israel's reception of that action on her behalf. God seems to be making a threefold comparison: His relationship in the covenant of salvation through the Messiah to earthly brides and bridegrooms, as well as to the priests and Israel. In this comparison, there is no discussion about what the ultimate reality is. There are only points of comparison among them. However, God's action is clearly the center of this text. It is also clear that this text is messianic and will find its final consummation only in the fulfillment of God's promise of salvation through the Messiah.

6. **How has the Messiah dressed His Bride in righteousness?**

____

____

____

____

7. **How are the comparisons in this text helpful in understanding our relationship with God?**

____

____

____

____

READ ISAIAH 62:1–5

Finally, in our investigation for this lesson, we look to these words from Isaiah 62:1–5:

1For Zion's sake I will not keep silent,
and for Jerusalem's sake I will not be quiet,
until her righteousness goes forth as brightness,
and her salvation as a burning torch.
2The nations shall see your righteousness,
and all kings your glory,
and you shall be called by a new name,
that the mouth of the Lord will give.
3You shall be a crown of beauty in the hand of the Lord,
and a royal diadem in the hand of your God.
4You shall no more be termed Forsaken,
and your land shall no more be termed Desolate,
but you shall be called My Delight Is in Her,
and your land Married;
for the Lord delights in you,
and your land shall be married.
5For as a young man marries a young woman,
so shall your sons marry you,
and as the bridegroom rejoices over the bride,
so shall your God rejoice over you.

The reason God will not hold His peace is because He wants the Bride's righteousness to shine. Salvation is the goal and promise of this text. The discussion of the marriage covenant is about the covenant of salvation that God is affirming to Israel. The Bride takes on a new name given to her by the Bridegroom when He marries her. This name is given because of the covenant of salvation she receives from Him. Her adornment includes a crown of glory. This is a theme repeated elsewhere in the Old Testament as God adorns her in His righteousness and glory. "The crown of life" (Revelation 2:10) is given by grace through faith. Instead of being called Forsaken, she is called My Delight Is in Her. Where the land was called Desolate, it is now called Married. All this results from the restoration God makes with Israel by His covenant of salvation. This clearly takes place in the fulfillment of the messianic promise, and this messianic context continues elsewhere in Scripture. This is a description of the marriage covenant of salvation that takes place when the Messiah restores Israel and adorns her with His righteousness. This is the cause for God's rejoicing. He rejoices in what He has given His Bride so that she is brought into His home and made His own. His joy is to see her dressed in glory.

8. **What do righteousness and salvation have to do with the changes and blessings that are described in Isaiah 62:2–12?**

____

____

____

____

9. Why were the name changes necessary?

____

____

____

____

10. What did God do to make those new names true for sinners like us?

____

____

____

____

REFLECTIONS ON GOD AND HIS PEOPLE

11. What do the texts from this lesson have in common?

____

____

____

____

12. How are the texts from this lesson different?

____

____

13. After working through this lesson, what have you learned about the marriage covenant of salvation? How would you apply these truths in marriage?

GOD'S RESPONSE TO ISRAEL'S SINFULNESS

This lesson looks primarily at texts where Israel was unfaithful and God called her to repent and promised to restore her when the Messiah came to earth to die for her sins. This is powerful imagery that is spoken in literal terms about the unfaithful wife and God's faithfulness to His covenant promises in the face of her unfaithfulness. He continually promised to restore Israel, which was intended to comfort her and is a great comfort to us.

GOD'S REALITY

JEREMIAH 2:2

2Go and proclaim in the hearing of Jerusalem, Thus says the LORD,

"I remember the devotion of your youth,
your love as a bride,
how you followed Me in the wilderness,
in a land not sown."

JEREMIAH 2:20

20“For long ago I broke your yoke
and burst your bonds;
but you said, ‘I will not serve.’
Yes, on every high hill
and under every green tree
you bowed down like a whore.”

JEREMIAH 3:1

1“If a man divorces his wife
and she goes from him
and becomes another man’s wife,
will he return to her?
Would not that land be greatly polluted?
You have played the whore with many lovers;
and would you return to Me?
declares the LORD.”

JEREMIAH 31:31–34

31Behold, the days are coming, declares the LORD, when
I will make a new covenant with the house of Israel
and the house of Judah, 32not like the covenant that I
made with their fathers on the day when I took them
by the hand to bring them out of the land of Egypt, My
covenant that they broke, though I was their husband,
declares the LORD. 33For this is the covenant that I will
make with the house of Israel after those days, declares
the LORD: I will put My law within them, and I will write

> it on their hearts. And I will be their God, and they shall be My people. [34]And no longer shall each one teach his neighbor and each his brother, saying, "Know the LORD," for they shall all know Me, from the least of them to the greatest, declares the LORD. For I will forgive their iniquity, and I will remember their sin no more.

Turning to Jeremiah 2–3, we begin a discussion of the other major scriptural emphasis on the marriage covenant of salvation in the Old Testament: Israel breaking the betrothal or marriage covenant by practicing idolatry. Jeremiah, and the other similar references in Scripture, refers to this as adultery or harlotry.

The discussion begins at Jeremiah 2:2, where God calls the prophet to cry out in the hearing of Jerusalem, "I remember the devotion of your youth, your love as bride, how you followed Me in the wilderness, in a land not sown." Here God affirms His marriage covenant with Israel. In 2:20, the prophet speaks of Israel's deliverance from bondage, in which Israel says she will not transgress but hypocritically play the prostitute everywhere. God condemns the idolatry that has brought her to the present crisis. She has deluded herself into believing that all is well when she has forgotten her Lord, or Bridegroom.

This is reinforced in 2:32, where Jeremiah prophesies, "Can a virgin forget her ornaments, or a bride her attire? Yet My people have forgotten Me days without number." Here God affirms that He is the ornament and attire of Israel. He has dressed her in His righteousness, but she has forsaken Him. The theme of her being dressed in Him will be repeated in the Old and New Testaments. The point of this section of Jeremiah is that despite this glorious dress in God's grace, God's people forsake Him with the harlotry of idolatry. The

Bride is so accused again in 3:1. God affirms that the Mosaic Law does not permit a man to remarry his divorced wife after her marriage to another man (Deuteronomy 24:1–4). But He calls Israel to return to Him. He will forgive and restore her when reason dictates that He should forsake her. This is a testimony to God's faithfulness in the covenant He has made with His people. While Israel repeatedly forsakes Him for others, He remains faithful in His covenant to redeem and save her.

This saving action is affirmed by God in Jeremiah 31:31–34. Here, He reminds His Bride of the covenant He made that she broke (v. 32). But He promises a new covenant, one of restoration in His relationship as her Husband, as He calls Himself in this text. This is clearly the covenant of salvation brought by the sending of the Messiah.

1. **In what sense was Israel's idolatry an act of spiritual adultery against God?**

____

____

____

____

2. **What does God speaking about being Israel's Husband have to do with the new covenant?**

____

____

____

READ EZEKIEL 16

The covenant relationship between God and Israel is graphically portrayed as a marriage in Ezekiel 16. God wants the prophet to indicate to Israel what her situation is in relation to His mercy. He describes her as forsaken at birth and left in her blood, with no one to have compassion on her. He sees her in her blood and calls her to life, making her grow to a mature age.

The language of this text affirms that the covenant relationship between God and His people is a covenant made by His grace. Everything in this text is His action. That this is the covenant of salvation and not the giving of the Law is further affirmed by the first action God takes. He covers her nakedness. This is an obvious reference to sin (see Genesis 3:6–11). His action on her behalf is to cover her sins. This language brings to mind the sacrifices instituted by God, especially the sacrifice of the lamb on the Day of Atonement. God covers the sins of the people with the blood of the lamb, foreshadowing the coming of the Lamb of God, who will cover them forever. He makes her His own by swearing an oath to her.

Then He dresses her, making her beautiful. She shines with His glory as His chosen Bride. She, who once was forsaken, is now known for the splendor she has received from Him. This language is congruent with the earlier prophecy of Isaiah 62, where the prophet describes this restoration. The point is that making her this way is God's action. His promised covenant of salvation has established Israel as His Bride.

Then the tone changes remarkably. God accuses her of trusting in her beauty and playing the prostitute by committing idolatry. He accuses her of taking all that He had done and making it the means of attracting her lovers. For this, He promises to gather her lovers and destroy them. He also asserts that she will suffer greatly for her actions. His words of condemnation almost reach the point of hopelessness. But then, at the end of chapter 16, God affirms His love and determination to fulfill the covenant He made with her. In this chapter, the prophet gives us the Word of God concerning the marriage covenant of salvation that God made with Israel, Israel broke and trampled, and God restored through the Messiah.

READ EZEKIEL 23

A similar discussion takes place in chapter 23. In this chapter, the two kingdoms (Judah and Israel) are depicted as sisters who belonged to God but played the prostitute by their idolatry. The condemnations heaped on them are similar to those in chapter 16. This chapter does not include any messianic promise of restoration. It reaffirms the marriage covenant God has with His people but sheds little light on much else.

3. **How is this true of the history of God and His people?**

___

___

___

___

4. **How do these texts speak to the issue of how these sexual sins help us understand the severity of our sins against God?**

___

___

5. **How does the harsh tone in this text add to the discussion of idolatry and sexual sins then and now?**

____

____

____

____

READ HOSEA 1–3

This brings us to a discussion of the opening chapters of the book of Hosea. God calls Hosea to be a prophet and commands him to marry an unfaithful woman because that is what Israel has been toward God (1:2). Children are born into this marriage and given names that point out how Israel has lost her relationship to God and how God has turned away from her. At the end of Hosea 1, God again affirms that He will restore and gather Israel, once again making her His own.

The heart of the problem is the same as in the other condemnation texts we have examined: namely, idolatry. God accuses her of breaking the First Commandment because she worshiped idols. This is harlotry against God, who made His eternal covenant with Israel.

God is faithful even when we are not. In Hosea 2, God reaffirms Israel by renaming her children "My people" and "You have received mercy" (v. 1), demonstrating His faithfulness to restore His people. He continues by calling Israel to repent, to put off her lovers. He pleads with her to see that her blessings have come from Him. He affirms the trials she will face for her sins but then promises to win her back. This is where the era of the Messiah comes in.

Again, we see the pattern prevalent in so many similar texts. Using imagery consistent with what we have heard so far, God uses the imagery of adultery by accusing Israel of unfaithfulness in His covenant relationship with her. God condemns this sin and promises to restore Israel by sending the Messiah. This text is unique because of the graphic acts that God calls the prophet to do to make His point. Such a marriage would normally have offended the children of Israel. But here, God points out her offense with a living reminder of her harlotry. He affirms this in Hosea 3 when the prophet buys the prostitute and makes her remain chaste—a shadow of the time when God will bring Israel back without a king. Then God will return her to Himself and David in the latter days. This is an obvious reference to the Messiah.

6. **How is Hosea's prophetic ministry different from most other prophets?**

____

____

____

____

7. **Why does God frequently change the names He gives His people in this section of Scripture?**

____

____

____

8. How, and when, does this happen in a Christian's life?

REFLECTIONS ON GOD AND HIS PEOPLE

9. What do these texts say about idolatry?

10. What do these texts say about God's faithfulness to us and our faithfulness to Him?

11. What might similar prophets say about idolatry and faithfulness in the church now?

____

____

____

____

12. What do these texts say about adultery? How do we apply that to the world we live in today, especially within the institution of marriage?

____

____

____

____

THE SONG OF SOLOMON

The Ephesians 5 of the Old Testament

This lesson is a journey into one of the most misunderstood and most wondrous books of the Bible: the Song of Solomon.

GOD'S REALITY

WHY IS THIS BOOK IN THE BIBLE?

Some believe that the Song of Solomon is nothing more than a series of love songs by Solomon and his bride. If that is all it is, it is fitting to question why it is included in Holy Scripture. How does it belong among the other works of the Old Testament?

The best way to determine why the Song of Solomon is included in Scripture is to see if other Old Testament works are similar in language to the Song of Solomon. We have already studied many texts that are written with the same terms as the Song of Solomon. The other references are to the marriage covenant of salvation, giving scriptural reasons for believing that the Song is as well. Since the language of the Song of Solomon keeps with the language in the others, we must conclude that the Song of Solomon is indeed a thorough look at the marriage covenant of salvation, foreshadowed in the love between Solomon and his bride. Because of the length and detail in this work, it is the most comprehensive lesson on the marriage covenant of salvation in the Old Testament. Solomon and his bride foreshadow Christ and the church, but, as we will learn in Ephesians 5, the relationship between the Christ and the church is the pattern we should follow when we get married.

WHO IS THE AUTHOR?

The author of this work is Solomon, son of David, king of Israel. It is a diary of love dialogue between Solomon and his beloved bride. The Song of Solomon covers the time before Solomon's wedding. Then it portrays the wedding itself and the relationship that continues over time.

As stated above, the book is also a reflection of the marriage covenant of salvation proclaimed in the Old Testament and fulfilled in Christ and the church. God and His Bride, the church, were preparing for when God would come to save her. It also foreshadows when God would fulfill His covenant promise in the incarnate God, Jesus Christ. Finally, it foreshadows when God and His people would live in the fulfillment. This includes both the church on earth and in heaven.

This work also testifies to fidelity before and during marriage as God-pleasing and beneficial to man. Part of the discussion of the marriage covenant of salvation includes the application made by God's people in their relationships. This work speaks of the faithfulness a man and a woman should have before and after their wedding. This faithfulness involves both chastity before and fidelity after the wedding. This faithfulness is a thankful response to the faithfulness of God in the marriage covenant He made with us, His people, in Christ.

THEMES IN THE SONG OF SOLOMON

MARRIAGE COVENANT OF SALVATION

The daughters of Jerusalem will witness the marriage of Solomon and his bride (see Song of Solomon 1:4). They are present in the Song of Solomon not only to see the events taking place but to bear witness to them. What they see becomes what is proclaimed.

In Luke 23:28, Jesus refers to the women lamenting for Him on the way to the cross as daughters of Jerusalem. They witness Jesus' suffering and death, which brings about God's covenant relationship with His people.

In Ephesians 5:22–33, a husband and wife are called to reflect the marriage covenant between Christ and the church. The marriage covenant of salvation teaches us how we come into this covenant relationship with God. It is also the example a married couple should follow in their marriage covenant. We will study this further in Lesson 8.

1. **Based on what we have read, how does the marriage covenant of salvation raise Christian marriage to a higher calling?**

____

____

____

____

FAITHFULNESS

Solomon and his bride were faithful to each other before and after their wedding. They lived chaste lives before the wedding, only expressing the intimacy of marriage after they were married.

God is faithful to His people, doing everything to make them His own and provide the environment for their faithfulness. The Old Testament establishes God's faithfulness to His covenant promise. The New Testament is the fulfillment of that promise in the crucifixion and resurrection of Jesus, followed by the relationship God and His people enjoy because of what Christ has done.

A husband and wife are called to faithfulness to God by being sexually faithful to each other before and after their wedding. This involves showing their faithfulness to God by abstaining from sex before their wedding. The covenant promise of faithfulness is made when God joins them in marriage and continues to be present in their faithful love of each other throughout marriage.

Read Song of Solomon 2:7; 3:5; 8:4.

2. **What do these words mean in relation to the discussion of faithfulness?**

____

____

____

____

GARDENS

In the consummation of the marriage between the bride and the groom, the bride is described as his locked (4:12) and then unlocked

(4:13–5:1) garden. There are several other references in the Song of Solomon to gardens.

This reminds us of the Garden of Eden, where marriage was instituted as a one-flesh union between one man and one woman (Genesis 2:18–24). Here God took the rib from Adam and made the woman to be “a helper fit for him” (v. 20). God instituted the marriage covenant of one flesh in Paradise not just as a means of keeping order but as the means by which a husband and wife should live in God’s love together.

This also reminds us of the garden where Jesus rose from the dead, pronouncing His marriage covenant of salvation complete. He sealed His covenant relationship to us by fulfilling God’s promise to make us His own by His death for our sins and by His resurrection.

3. **What do these garden references mean in relation to our discussion of the Song of Solomon?**

____

____

____

____

INITIATION AND RECEPTION

Solomon initiates the relationship between himself and his bride, as well as the marriage (Song of Solomon 3:6–11). His bride joyfully receives his love and responds with her love for him (see 1:4).

Likewise, Jesus initiates salvation (John 3:16–17). He comes in love, suffers, dies, and rises to make us His own. We receive His loving grace and respond by confessing our love for Him.

4. **How can this be reflected by Christian men and women before and during marriage?**

YEARNING AND CONSUMMATION

Solomon and his bride yearn for each other in anticipation of being married. This is not a sinful yearning but one that is faithful to God's Word since they remain sexually faithful before marriage. Yearning is natural but can be godly or sinful based on whether God's clearly expressed will is kept.

In like manner, Jesus yearns for Jerusalem, whom He has come to save (Matthew 23:37–39). The blessings of that salvation will come by faith in Him as the Savior.

5. **What is the difference between yearning or attraction and lust?**

6. **Why does God forbid sexual intercourse apart from marriage? (See Genesis 2:18–24; Matthew 19:1–6.)**

____

____

____

____

____

REFLECTIONS ON GOD AND HIS PEOPLE

7. **How does the part of the Song of Solomon before Solomon and his wife's wedding remind us of the Old Testament times, the present times, or both?**

____

____

____

____

8. **How does Solomon's wedding remind us of the coming of Christ in the New Testament or His return?**

____

____

____

9. How does the period after Solomon's wedding remind us of today or of heaven?

____

____

____

____

____

____

10. What does the Song of Solomon teach us about our relationship to God?

____

____

____

____

____

11. How do those lessons apply to your marriage?

____

____

____

____

____

12. What can people who are dating or preparing for marriage learn from the Song of Solomon?

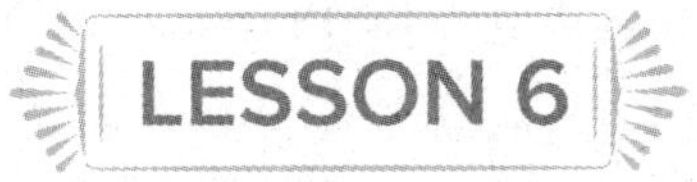

MARRIAGE COVENANT LANGUAGE IN THE GOSPELS

The culmination of the marriage covenant of salvation is the coming of the heavenly Bridegroom, Jesus, the Son of God. This lesson demonstrates the marriage covenant language found in the four Gospels.

GOD'S REALITY

MATTHEW 9:15

The first example of this is in Matthew 9:15, with parallel passages in Mark 2:19–20 and Luke 5:34–35. Matthew records these words of Jesus: "Can the wedding guests mourn as long as the bridegroom is with them? The days will come when the bridegroom is taken away from them, and then they will fast." These words follow John's question: "Why do we and the Pharisees fast, but Your disciples do not fast?" (v. 14).

What is to be learned from this regarding the marriage covenant of salvation? Some may argue that it has nothing to do with it at all.

They would maintain that Jesus is just using an example that everyone understood. That argument has validity if you take these words apart from the context of what the Old Testament teaches. There are, however, major problems with this. Jesus continually points out how He fulfills the Scripture. He alludes to Old Testament images in reference after reference. To assume that He is not pointing back to what the Scriptures say about the marriage covenant of salvation is to make this an exception to the vast number of references where He clearly implies or states that He fulfills the Old Testament (e.g., Mark 14:49; Luke 4:21).

That Jesus is the Bridegroom promised in the Old Testament marriage imagery and that His mission is to be "taken away from them," which refers to His death and subsequent resurrection, contributes to the discussion of the marriage covenant of salvation in this passage. Jesus clearly affirms that He is the Bridegroom. He identifies Himself as the fulfillment of God's promise. He also affirms that this is going to be an event unlike any other. There will be a time of incredible grief. This grief will be caused by the fact that He is taken away (in death). Here, He does not go on to point out the unending joy that will follow. Jesus clearly points out that He is the Bridegroom in this parable, a truth which He ties to what He came to do.

1. **Is there any question that Jesus is the Bridegroom in this parable? Why or why not?**

____

____

____

2. **Who are the "wedding guests"?**

____

____

____

____

MATTHEW 12:39; 16:4

Jesus again employs the language of the Old Testament when He says in Matthew 12:39, "An evil and adulterous generation seeks for a sign, but no sign will be given to it except the sign of the prophet Jonah."

He expresses the same in Matthew 16:4: "An evil and adulterous generation seeks for a sign, but no sign will be given to it except the sign of Jonah."

This is a clear reference to the similar adultery language God used in the Old Testament to condemn Israel for her idolatry and unbelief. Jesus affirms that the same conditions exist in these New Testament people that previously existed in those He condemned in the writings of the prophets. He states that nothing has changed in Israel. Israel of old had practiced adultery against God by rejecting Him, and the Jewish leaders were doing it again. In both of the texts from Matthew that are listed above, the leaders ask Jesus to perform a sign to validate His words. He gives them the same sign in both cases: the sign of Jonah—namely, His death and resurrection. They also deny this, thus confirming for eternity their spiritual adultery. By rejecting Jesus, the Jewish leaders continue the spiritual adultery Israel was guilty of in the Old Testament.

Jesus uses the same terms in Mark 8:38, where He says, "For whoever is ashamed of Me and of My words in this adulterous and sinful generation, of him will the Son of Man also be ashamed when He comes in the glory of His Father with the holy angels." These words are far more personal. Jesus does not just condemn the attitude of the leaders of the Jews; He deals with individuals participating in this adultery. Jesus indicts the generation of His day by referencing the time when Israel broke the marriage covenant of salvation in the Old Testament. He condemns those who participate in this spiritual adultery by denying God's Messiah as well as joining themselves to an idol of law and meaningless ceremonies. This affirms that the marriage covenant of salvation is just as real, if not more so, in Jesus' day as it had been before.

3. **How are these words similar to those in the Old Testament?**

____

____

____

____

4. **How did the people Jesus condemned commit adultery or idolatry?**

____

____

____

____

READ MATTHEW 22:1–14; 25:1–13

Our investigation now turns to two parables Jesus told that refer to a wedding. The first is the parable of the wedding feast in Matthew 22:1–14; the second is in Matthew 25:1–13. What is the significance of these parables as it relates to the image of the marriage between God and His people? First, both parables assume Jesus to be the Bridegroom and that these weddings have to do with salvation. There does not seem to be any controversy about who the Bridegroom is in these parables. Jesus obviously refers to Himself. In doing so, He identifies Himself as the promised fulfillment of the Old Testament marriage texts—who is the Messiah. In addition, in both parables, Jesus identifies those who are brought into the kingdom of God and those who are not. So, Jesus affirms both Himself as the heavenly Bridegroom, whom God sent, and the fact that this marriage is associated with salvation.

5. **What is the common occasion in these two texts?**

____

____

____

____

6. **What does it mean to be locked out of this event?**

____

____

____

____

JOHN 2:1–11

> [1]On the third day there was a wedding at Cana in Galilee, and the mother of Jesus was there. [2]Jesus also was invited to the wedding with His disciples. [3]When the wine ran out, the mother of Jesus said to Him, "They have no wine." [4]And Jesus said to her, "Woman, what does this have to do with Me? My hour has not yet come." [5]His mother said to the servants, "Do whatever He tells you."
>
> [6]Now there were six stone water jars there for the Jewish rites of purification, each holding twenty or thirty gallons. [7]Jesus said to the servants, "Fill the jars with water." And they filled them up to the brim. [8]And He said to them, "Now draw some out and take it to the master of the feast." So they took it. [9]When the master of the feast tasted the water now become wine, and did not know where it came from (though the servants who had drawn the water knew), the master of the feast called the bridegroom [10]and said to him, "Everyone serves the good wine first, and when people have drunk freely, then the poor wine. But you have kept the good wine until now."

In this text, Jesus asks His mother, "Woman, what does this have to do with Me? My hour has not yet come" (v. 4). What is the hour He is referring to? Is it the hour to begin His ministry? Apparently not, since that began in John 1. Is it the hour to do miracles? Apparently not, because He proceeds to do one. There are many references in John to Jesus' "hour." Most, if not all, of those refer to His hour to suffer and die. This text also seems to refer to His suffering and death. The connection is to the Old Testament texts where God promises to fulfill His marriage covenant of salvation in the mission of the Messiah, the Suffering Servant. In asking Him to provide the wine, Jesus' mother calls on Him to do what the bridegroom at the wedding is responsible for doing: providing food and wine for the feast. His answer may remind her that He would fulfill the promised marriage covenant of salvation, providing the ultimate feast through His suffering, death, and rising again. The miracle of changing water to wine then points to the greater miracle that would one day be accomplished by His atoning sacrifice.

7. When did Jesus provide the feast?

____

____

____

____

8. How did He accomplish this?

____

____

____

____

READ JOHN 3

The Gospel of John identifies Jesus as the Bridegroom in the words of John the Baptist: "The one who has the bride is the bridegroom. The friend of the bridegroom, who stands and hears Him, rejoices greatly at the bridegroom's voice. Therefore this joy of mine is now complete" (John 3:29).

This verse falls within the context of John's disciples pointing out that Jesus is commanding larger crowds than John. John affirms that Jesus is the heavenly Bridegroom promised by the prophets. John not only points out that Jesus is the Messiah, but he also affirms that the mission of the Messiah is to give God's people eternal life. This is asserted before this verse in John 3:16 and after in John 3:36. In John 3:29, Jesus is affirmed as the Messiah, the Bridegroom promised to Israel as her Redeemer.

9. What did John the Baptist prepare the people for?

____

____

____

____

10. What does John the Baptist preparing people have to do with the marriage covenant of salvation?

____

____

____

REFLECTIONS ON GOD AND HIS PEOPLE

11. How do these texts show the marriage covenant of salvation fulfilled in Jesus?

12. What facets of ancient marriage customs do we see in these texts?

13. How does Jesus affirming that He is the Bridegroom help us understand the Old Testament marriage texts?

MARRIAGE COVENANT LANGUAGE IN THE EPISTLES AND REVELATION

The Epistles and Revelation apply the teachings of the Old Testament to Jesus. Many of these texts are familiar but are not always seen as applications of Old Testament teaching. Consider these texts in the context of what you have already read.

GOD'S REALITY

ROMANS 7:1–6

1Or do you not know brothers—for I am speaking to those
who know the law—that the law is binding on a person
as long as he lives? 2For a married woman is bound by
law to her husband while he lives, but if her husband
dies she is released from the law of marriage.

3Accordingly, she will be called an adulteress if she lives
with another man while her husband is alive. But if her
husband dies, she is free from that law, and if she marries another man she is not an adulteress.

> [4]Likewise, my brothers, you also have died to the law through the body of Christ, so that you may belong to another, to Him who was raised from the dead, in order that we may bear fruit for God. [5]For while we were living in the flesh, our sinful passions, aroused by the law, were at work in our members to bear fruit to death. [6]But now we are released from the law, having died to that which held us captive, so that we serve in the new way of the Spirit and not in the old way of the written code.

How does this contribute to our discussion? Paul also discusses dying with Christ and being made new in His resurrection in Romans 6:3–4. He uses the example of a married woman being bound to her husband until he dies—when she is free to marry. He affirms that she would be an adulteress if she married again while she was already married. He then affirms that we, who were bound by the Law, have been set free from the Law through Christ. He affirms that we are united to Christ in the Gospel. Paul confirms that the Old Testament concept of the marriage covenant of salvation is fulfilled in the church's relationship to Christ. He also affirms that the fruit of this marriage is produced by the Spirit through the Gospel, not by the Law.

How do we know that he is speaking of the church and not of individuals? While death to the Law and freedom in Christ is true of individual members, Paul addresses them corporately in the plural. He asserts this truth for the church, which also applies to individual children of God. Referring to individuals as children of God seems to be a trend in Paul's writings, while he speaks of the church in terms of marriage to Christ. In this text, the truth he states is addressed to the church while also being true of each member. The language of this text is similar to the various Old Testament prophets who called Israel a prostitute while affirming God's marriage to Israel.

Is this simply an example and, therefore, not an affirmation of the marriage covenant image of Christ and the church? It is possible. However, to come to such a conclusion isolates this reference to marriage and Christ from the rest of what Paul says on the subject, specifically in Ephesians 5:22–33. There is nothing in this context to indicate that Paul is not affirming the marriage of Christ and the church. Since he so eloquently discusses that marriage elsewhere, we would naturally conclude that this is at least a veiled affirmation of the marriage between Christ and the church, which is clearly taught in the Old Testament. The major point bears repeating: the marriage between Christ and the church is the Gospel. It is freedom from the Law. It is accomplished by His death. This falls beautifully within the context of the scriptural teaching concerning the marriage of God.

1. **What is the dying and new marriage in this text?**

____

____

____

____

COLOSSIANS 3:18–19

18 Wives, submit to your husbands, as is fitting in the Lord.

19 Husbands, love your wives, and do not be harsh with them.

Here, Paul gently reminds the church in Colossae of a greater teaching, especially if the letter to the Ephesians had been previously read to them. We will examine how Paul uses the words "submit" and "love" in our discussion of Ephesians 5.

2. **How do these words help you understand roles within marriage? What questions do they raise?**

____

____

____

____

HEBREWS 13:4

> [4]Let marriage be held in honor among all, and let the marriage bed be undefiled, for God will judge the sexually immoral and adulterous.

This text is very helpful in our present circumstances where the existence of and need for marriage is questioned by many in our society. This text, though, also affirms that sexual intercourse in the covenant of marriage should only be between a husband and his wife. In a time when Christians are compromising this teaching in large numbers, this passage from the book of Hebrews confirms God's will. This teaching should remain an important component of what we teach and practice.

3. **What defiles the marriage bed?**

____

____

____

1 PETER 3:1–7

> 1 Likewise, wives, be subject to your own husbands,
> so that even if some do not obey the word, they may
> be won without a word by the conduct of their wives,
> 2 when they see your respectful and pure conduct. 3 Do
> not let your adorning be external—the braiding of hair
> and the putting on of gold jewelry, or the clothing you
> wear—4 but let your adorning be the hidden person of
> the heart with the imperishable beauty of a gentle and
> quiet spirit, which in God's sight is very precious. 5 For
> this is how the holy women who hoped in God used to
> adorn themselves, by submitting to their own husbands,
> 6 as Sarah obeyed Abraham, calling him lord. And you
> are her children, if you do good and do not fear any-
> thing that is frightening.
>
> 7 Likewise, husbands, live with your wives in an under-
> standing way, showing honor to the woman as the
> weaker vessel, since they are heirs with you of the grace
> of life, so that your prayers may not be hindered.

This text affirms the primary role of a male in a marriage. When we consider the other texts referenced in this lesson, we understand that this relationship is derived from the accountability Jesus took for the sins of His Bride, the church. His reference to wives as "the weaker vessel" seems to be a reference to physical strength and stature, not to dignity or worth in the eyes of God.

4. Why do males have greater accountability in the marriage covenant?

____

____

____

____

READ REVELATION 17

Our investigation of the marriage covenant between Christ and His church moves to the book of Revelation. Revelation 17 speaks of the "prostitute." The language in Revelation 17 is very similar to the words found in Ezekiel and Hosea in which God describes Israel as having played the prostitute by chasing after idols. Where this language differs from those Old Testament references is the definition of who the prostitute is. In the Old Testament, the prostitute represents Israel, or the church, who has forsaken God. God calls her to repentance and restoration through various means. The point is clear: this is Israel who will be restored by her heavenly Bridegroom, the Messiah. Revelation 17 differs from the Old Testament passages already mentioned in this study in that the prostitute is not the church. Here, in the New Testament, the prostitute pretends to be the church but is not. She is not because she does not receive the grace that comes from Christ. She does not affirm His death and resurrection as the bond that seals her to Him. She does not cling to His promises but seeks to replace Him in many ways as the Head of the church. She looks appealing. She appears to be what so many assume the church would be. But she is a prostitute because she is not married to the heavenly Bridegroom.

5. How is this language like that of the Old Testament prophets?

____

____

____

____

6. What false teachings threaten the church today?

____

____

____

____

READ REVELATION 19

Next we read Revelation 19, which is a celebration of salvation. The church triumphant praises God for His work of salvation. He is praised in His mighty power for saving His people. In the context of that celebration, we find verse 7: "Let us rejoice and exult and give Him the glory, for the marriage of the Lamb has come, and His Bride has made herself ready."

This text raises many points of interest. The first is the marriage of the Lamb. The Old Testament speaks of the marriage of God and Israel as the covenant of salvation. John identifies Jesus as the Lamb of God (John 1:29, 36; Revelation 5:6; 7:17) and as the heavenly Bridegroom (John 3:29). Considered together, these references clearly point to the coming of the Messiah and the fulfilling of His mission: to be the atoning Lamb of God, who fulfills the role of the heavenly Bridegroom.

Revelation 19:8 continues, "'It was granted her to clothe herself with fine linen, bright and pure'—for the fine linen is the righteous deeds of the saints." This continues the ideas expressed in verse 7. The new aspect of this verse is the righteous deeds of the saints. This fine linen is the dressing from Christ, who has freed and empowered His Bride to show forth righteous deeds. This interpretation is consistent with the language found throughout Scripture.

The text continues in verse 9: "The angel said to me, 'Write this: "Blessed are those who are invited to the marriage supper of the Lamb."'" This is a unique biblical concept. The text had been speaking of the Bride of Christ. It now speaks of those invited, the members of that Bride. The saints make up the Bride, who is dressed by God in the righteous deeds He has empowered her members to perform. Here we have an example of the weaving of two biblical teachings: the teaching that the church is the Bride of Christ, and the teaching that the church is the Body of Christ are inseparable. (See Ephesians 5:23.) This is the essence of the "one flesh" of Christ and His Bride. She is His Bride, and she is His Body. Her members are His. This is true because He has made it so by His death and resurrection. He took what was hers and made it His. Then He took what was His and made it hers. He took her sins to Himself as His own and dressed her in His glorious righteousness (2 Corinthians 5:21).

7. **What is the marriage feast of the Lamb?**

____

____

____

READ REVELATION 21

The final text we will discuss in this chapter is Revelation 21:2: "And I saw the holy city, new Jerusalem, coming down out of heaven from God, prepared as a bride adorned for her husband." The first thing that comes to mind is the similar language used in Isaiah 54. Both texts refer to the image of the marriage covenant between God and His people. Both texts also refer to a new Jerusalem. The Old Testament concept of the covenant of salvation as described as a marriage between God and His people is validated in this text. In Revelation, John links the messianic promises to the person and work of Jesus.

The key concept of this verse that supports the importance of this text for tracing the teaching of the church as the Bride of Christ is that the new Jerusalem is prepared as a bride adorned for her husband. The application of Old Testament texts has been pointed out in the discussion of Revelation 19. There is nothing about this text that contradicts the other sections of Scripture on the image of the marriage of God to His Bride, the church. Rather, this text affirms the prior teaching as it presents the fulfillment of the messianic mission: the total preparation of the Bride for eternal bliss in Jesus' presence. This has been accomplished by Jesus' death and resurrection and will be fulfilled in the resurrection on the Last Day.

8. How is the new Jerusalem the Bride of Christ?

____

____

____

____

9. What is her adornment?

REFLECTIONS ON GOD AND HIS PEOPLE

10. What connection do these texts have with the Old Testament covenant of salvation?

11. How are the actions of God's people a reflection of that covenant?

EPHESIANS 5

The Song of Solomon of the New Testament

Ephesians 5:22–33 is clearly the most read marriage text in Scripture. In this lesson, you will read it and discuss it in its immediate context and the context of the rest of the biblical teaching about the marriage covenant of salvation.

GOD'S REALITY

> [22]Wives, submit to your own husbands, as to the Lord.
> [23]For the husband is the head of the wife even as Christ
> is the head of the church, His body, and is Himself its
> Savior. [24]Now as the church submits to Christ, so also
> wives should submit in everything to their husbands.
>
> [25]Husbands, love your wives, as Christ loved the church
> and gave Himself up for her, [26]that He might sancti-
> fy her, having cleansed her by the washing of water
> with the word, [27]so that He might present the church
> to Himself in splendor, without spot or wrinkle or any

> such thing, that she might be holy and without blemish.
> 28In the same way husbands should love their wives as
> their own bodies. He who loves his wife loves himself.
> 29For no one ever hated his own flesh, but nourishes and
> cherishes it, just as Christ does the church, 30because we
> are members of His body. 31"Therefore a man shall leave
> his father and mother and hold fast to his wife, and the
> two shall become one flesh." 32This mystery is profound,
> and I am saying that it refers to Christ and the church.
> 33However, let each one of you love his wife as himself,
> and let the wife see that she respects her husband.

WIDER CONTEXT: VERSES 1–2

In these verses, we are called to be imitators of God. God is our heavenly Father. It is natural for children to imitate their fathers, but it is unnatural for us to think we can play God. Therefore, Paul calls us by faith to imitate the love, kindness, and mercy we have seen in God.

The love of God in Christ's sacrifice on the cross is the ultimate example. Christ completely gave of Himself for us. We have come to know the mind of God in Jesus' sacrifice of Himself for our salvation.

The rest of the lesson shows us first how not to do that, and then how to do it. We will look at the specifics Paul employs in both. Ultimately, what Paul affirms is not intended to be a burden of Law but a calling in the grace of Christ. We are called away from the base fixation of the flesh to something higher.

VERSES 3–21

This section contrasts the sins that are a contradiction to imitating God and the things that truly imitate God. Some suggest that the sexual sins referred to in this context are different from those in the world today. There is no textual reason to believe this. Sexual sins have not substantively changed over time. What Paul condemns in this text is still being practiced today. These sexual sins are particularly cited as being contrary to imitating God. It is idolatrous to practice sexual sins and indulge in sinful desires. When we decide that we know how to live better than the way God has told us in His Word we should live, we commit idolatry by making ourselves and our wisdom greater than God. This reference to idolatry also reminds us of the texts we studied in Ezekiel 16 and 23, where Israel's idolatry was also called adultery. The biblical connection between sexual sins and idolatry appears in both the Old and New Testaments, and the comparison goes both ways. Sexual sins are a confession in action that contradicts the marriage covenant of salvation. Sexual activity before marriage among Christians is a confession of action that asserts that God enters into a covenant with us apart from His promises, which He never does. When Christians commit adultery, it gives other people the impression that God is unfaithful. But He never is. Homosexuality is a confession of action that implies God loves Himself, not us. This is no doubt not the understanding of those living in these relationships. Very often, in our sinfulness, we confess what we don't intend. God, who created us, knows us better than we know ourselves. Willful sin, whether intentionally or not, implies that we know what is good and right better than God does.

In contrast, this section affirms that the general way to imitate God is through thanksgiving, walking in the light, singing hymns, and so on. Where sexual sins tear down and destroy, imitating God builds and edifies. We are called away from the sexual fixation of the world to those holy practices and attitudes that affirm God's covenant with us.

VERSES 22–33

In this section, Paul does not explain that there is a marriage covenant of salvation. He instead seems to assume that the Ephesian readers and hearers already know this based, we would suppose, on the various texts in the Old Testament. He affirms that the Old Testament covenant of salvation refers to Christ and the church. Then he applies this covenant to a husband and wife. Imitating Christ is a calling, not simply a response to the Law.

It is important to realize the point of comparison in this section. Many assume that Paul is comparing the covenant of salvation to marriage. The opposite is true. In this text, Paul uses the powerful image of Christ and the church to help married couples understand their calling as a husband or wife. Paul makes that clear at the end of this section when he points out that the main truth in marriage is actually Christ and the church, but this also applies to a husband and wife.

Paul points to the reality of the marriage covenant of salvation; this marriage covenant is the Gospel. While Paul commands a husband to love his wife, the example he uses is the Gospel. Paul's retelling of what Christ did in love for us is one of the most complete presentations of the Gospel anywhere in Scripture. He affirms Christ's sacrifice for our sins, the cleansing from sin we receive in Baptism, and the dressing of His Bride, the church, in His righteousness. In this Gospel context, Jesus is the true definition of a husband.

It is this Gospel example that husbands are called to follow. A husband is called to reflect the love of Christ (in the Gospel) to his wife. That love is, by definition, sacrificial and complete. The notion of a fifty-fifty marriage falls away in the light of the marriage covenant of salvation, where Christ gives everything, including His life, to make His Bride His own. A man is called to completely love his wife, just as Jesus completely loves us. Jesus has defined what it means to be a husband, and men are called to live out that definition in love.

The primary submission of the church to Jesus in the Gospel is the reception of His loving sacrifice for her. What she does is a response to what she receives. The church, therefore, is the definition of a wife.

Women are called to reflect the reception of Jesus' love by the church. The primary subjection of a Christian wife is not what she does but what she receives. What she does is a response to what she receives. That response is also total, as a husband's love is for his wife. Thus, instead of a fifty-fifty relationship, Christian marriage is a one hundred-one hundred relationship. A woman is exemplified by the church and her loving response to the love of Jesus. A woman is to receive her husband's love and respond by loving him in return through the respect she shows him.

REFLECTIONS ON GOD AND HIS PEOPLE

1. **What does a Christian's participation in sexual sins wrongly imply about God and His covenant with us?**

2. **In Paul's comparison of Christ and the church to a husband and wife, how does Paul show that a marriage between a man and a woman reflects the relationship between Christ and the church?**

3. **What is the church's response to the loving sacrifice Jesus made for us? What does that look like in congregational life?**

4. **In this calling, what is the motivation for your conduct as a husband or wife?**

5. **What do these relationships look like in your home?**

6. **Why is it important for a man to love his wife and for a woman to respect her husband?**

LEADER GUIDE

LESSON 1

THE COVENANT OF SALVATION

OPENING NOTE: It is difficult to predict what the word *covenant* will mean to people participating in this study. That's fine. The focus of this lesson is to help learners understand the covenant of salvation God has made with us. If the covenants they know about are different from that one, be prepared to point out the difference between human covenants and our covenant relationship with God.

1. **What kind of covenant has God made with us? How does this differ from covenants, commitments, and contracts we make in the world?**

   How much time you take on these texts is something you can determine in the moment. Some may not need to spend much time at all, while others (likely those quite unfamiliar with covenants) may simply look at these texts and move on (there will be application in the questions below). Have them discuss the Old Testament covenants.

   - Read about the covenant of circumcision in Genesis 17:1–14.

Circumcision: God commanded that the foreskins of the male members of Israel be cut off on the eighth day (the day of the new creation). This was fulfilled when Jesus' blood was shed to bring about the new creation.

- Read about the Passover covenant in Exodus 13:3–16.

Passover: The blood of the male lamb was shed and then placed on the doorposts and lintel. When the angel of death saw the blood, he passed by that house. Jesus' blood was shed when He died in our place. Death no longer has dominion over us because of His death and resurrection.

- Read about the covenant made on the Day of Atonement in Leviticus 16.

The Day of Atonement: The sins of the people were loaded onto the scapegoat, and the goat was chased out into the wilderness to bear away the sins of the people. The spotless male lamb was killed. The high priest took the blood into the Most Holy Place and sprinkled it on the mercy seat, covering the sins of the people. Then the priest went out and sprinkled the blood on the people, assuring them that their sins were atoned for. Jesus atoned for our sins on the cross. He carried our sins to Calvary and shed His blood for us. We are cleansed by His blood.

____

____

2. How does the covenant God made with us differ from covenants we have made with others?

The major difference between the covenant God made with us and those we make with others in this world is that God is the one who accomplishes every aspect of our covenant with Him, whereas earthly covenants tend to have action by both parties to fulfill the covenant.

You may want to discuss covenants in and out of the church. The three major covenants we experience in our life in the church are the following:

Baptism: This is a covenant God made with us in which He forgives our sins (Acts 2:38), gives us salvation (Romans 6:1–4; 1 Peter 3:21), and grants the gift of faith by the Holy Spirit (Acts 2:38; Titus 3:4–7).

Confirmation: This is not instituted by God. Confirmation is when we confess the faith into which we were baptized. We acknowledge, by faith, the one-sided covenant God made with us.

*Marriage: This is God joining husband and wife together in the marriage covenant that reflects His marriage covenant with us. The vows are first spoken to God, then to each other. You may want to have the Rite of Holy Matrimony (*Lutheran Service Book, *pp. 275–77) handy to read to participants. Ask them to identify which vows are spoken to God and which are spoken between husband and wife.*

You may want them to discuss (as the participants are comfortable) various contracts or other covenants they might have made with others.

---

3. **What is God's covenant based on? What does this mean in our relationship to Him?**

   God's covenant is based on His love and mercy. In His justice, the price for sin (death) had to be paid. God foreshadowed His solution in the saving events of the Old Testament, the sacrifices, and the words of mercy spoken through the prophets. All was fulfilled in Jesus' life, suffering, death, and resurrection. God's love and mercy are embodied in Jesus, and we receive the blessings of salvation by God's grace through faith. Our relationship with Him, therefore, is one of reception followed by a response. We receive His grace (undeserved favor) and respond with thanksgiving and praise, which is expressed in word and deed.

   ____

   ____

   ____

   ____

   ____

   ____

4. **Based on our understanding of God's covenant with us, what does it mean to center our lives on Christ?**

   We hear this expression (Christ-centered) often, but there seems to be a significant difference in what it means. It is sometimes used in a generic sense (such as the speculation "What would Jesus do?"). To be truly Christ-centered is to focus on what Jesus did that made us His own. We focus on His sacrificial death and His resurrection.

   ____

   ____

   ____

   ____

   ____

5. **Similarly, what does it mean to center our relationships on Christ?**

   The same applies. Our relationships are centered on Jesus' sacrifice for us. We live in the same sacrificial love He has shown us by His loving actions on our behalf.

   ____

   ____

   ____

   ____

   ____

6. **Most importantly for this conversation, what does it mean to center marriage on Christ?**

   This is perhaps the covenant relationship that most mirrors God's relationship to us in Christ. We will continually discuss how our relationship as a husband or wife reflects our relationship with God in Christ.

7. **What is different about your view of covenant relationships after reading through this lesson?**

   See if participants look at covenants any differently because of this brief discussion. They may not.

8. **What do you hope to find in the following lessons to help you understand how our covenant relationship with God affects our relationships?**

   Answers will vary. Some may not have any idea. Others may have specific things they would like to learn.

   ____

   ____

   ____

   ____

   ____

   ____

LEADER GUIDE

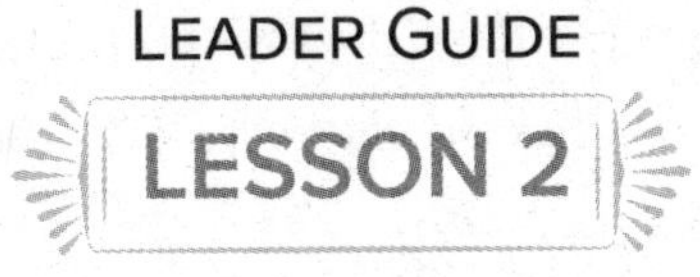

DEFINITIONS

OPENING NOTE: The definitions discussed here are radically different from everything we are told in society, including possible definitions from fellow Christians. Be patient, allowing these biblical definitions to sink in.

1. **What different definitions of love do you encounter? What's wrong with the false ones? How do those definitions fall short of truly fulfilling people's lives?**

   Take the time to let participants relate the various definitions of love they encounter. Lead them to evaluate those definitions based on God's love for us.

   ____

   ____

   ____

   ____

   ____

2. **Where do we go to find a true definition of the word *love*? Why? What does it mean that God is love? What does that have to do with the cross?**

   True love is best defined by Jesus' death and resurrection. God has defined it as such. God is, in His essence, love. Love caused Him to create all things (Psalm 136). When humanity fell away, love caused Him to promise salvation. His love finds its culmination at the cross. (See John 3:16–17.)

   ____

   ____

   ____

   ____

3. **What is the role of self-sacrifice in love? How do we know that? How can you show the self-sacrificial love of Jesus to people in your life? Be specific.**

   Love, in Scripture, is seldom described as an emotion. It is almost always described as God's action toward us. That loving action is self-sacrificial, especially the defining act of Jesus' death and resurrection. (See 1 John 4:1–11.) Lead participants to discuss how they show this love now and how they might show it in new ways in the future.

   ____

   ____

   ____

   ____

4. **Why should you show love to others? Where is that love centered (on others or yourself)? Whom has God given you to love? How can you center your love on them? Be specific.**

   Our motivation for showing love is the love we have received from God, specifically Jesus' gift of grace to us. True love is always centered on the one being loved. Lead participants in a discussion of the privilege they have to show His love to people in their lives (as they are comfortable).

   ___

   ___

   ___

5. **Is love an obligation or a privilege? What does that mean when you show it? How does it affect your attitude? Whom has God given you the privilege to love? How do you desire to show those people Christ? Be specific.**

   The Law shows us our obligations. Love is the privilege to show God's love (doing what the Law requires because of the love we have received). By living by faith and in His love, we do the things the Law requires with little or no regard for the requirement. Lead participants in a discussion about how to love people in their lives with the sacrificial love of Christ (as they are comfortable).

   ___

   ___

   ___

   ___

6. **What is the world's view of authority? How is it flawed? What examples of bad use of authority in the workplace can you give? What examples can you give of bad use of authority in society or in government?**

   The world's view of authority is primarily power and perks. This view does not raise others, nor does it encourage productivity, but it demands simple obedience. Lead participants to discuss (as they are comfortable) examples in their lives.

   ____

   ____

   ____

   ____

7. **What abuse of authority takes place in the home? What is wrong with these examples of people abusing their authority? What attitudes lead to such abuse of authority? What happens to lives and relationships with this flawed definition of authority in the home?**

   Viewing authority in the home as the world does leads to dictatorship, fear, mistrust, and isolation. Too often, other abuse is quick to follow. That kind of exercise of authority is inherently selfish. True love is not selfish.

   ____

   ____

   ____

   ____

8. **How did Jesus define authority in Mark 9:33–37? How did He enhance this point in Matthew 20:20–28? What did He teach His disciples in John 13:1–20?**

Authority is service. Love serves, and service builds, raises, and empowers. Jesus left the disciples in charge with the call to loving service. His love has served the church for centuries.

____

____

____

____

____

9. **What authority does Jesus have? See Matthew 28:18. How does He exercise that authority? How does Jesus' death and resurrection define authority?**

Jesus has all authority in heaven and earth. He exercises His authority by self-sacrificial loving service. The greatest authoritative act of all time was His death and resurrection for us. It, therefore, serves as the defining authoritative act.

____

____

____

____

____

10. Why should we adopt the definition of authority used in this lesson? How does it express our faith? How can a Christian boss confess his or her faith through his or her business? How can people in authority lead those in their care to greater achievement?

The definition of authority in this lesson is God's definition. It is our calling as God's people, fulfilled in the love He has given us. It is an expression of our faith in that it shows the love He demonstrated on the cross. Lead participants into a discussion of how this should work in various callings in life.

____

____

____

____

11. What is authority? How does this definition of authority call you to change? How can you confess your faith in the way you exercise your authority? How will this definition of authority change lives and relationships?

Authority is service. Lead participants to discuss how this affects the positions of authority they hold and how it affects what they look for in those who exercise it over them. How they serve while being under authority is also vital and shows the humility and love of Christ to people over them.

____

____

LEADER GUIDE

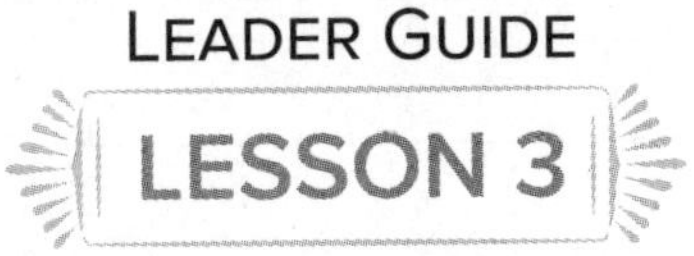

THE OLD TESTAMENT MARRIAGE COVENANT AFFIRMED

1. Why does it matter whether God is the King in this psalm?

It matters whether this is about the marriage covenant of salvation and has application to our relationship with God in that covenant. Based on the rest of Scripture, it makes sense that it is.

2. What is taking place in this psalm?

This psalm uses the imagery of a marriage ceremony between a king and his bride to teach us about the relationship we have with God through Jesus Christ.

____

____

3. What is the context of Isaiah 53?

Isaiah 53 precedes Isaiah 54:4–8. In the New Testament, Isaiah 53 is the most quoted Old Testament chapter. The context is Jesus accomplishing our salvation. Isaiah 53 speaks specifically about the Suffering Servant being "pierced for our transgressions" and "crushed for our iniquities" (v. 5). Isaiah 53 is clearly speaking of Jesus' death for our sins. This is the focus of the various New Testament references to it. The Redeemer spoken of in Isaiah 54 is the Suffering Servant in Isaiah 53.

____

____

____

____

____

4. Who is the husband in this text?

Yahweh, the Creator and Redeemer, refers to Himself as the husband. The covenant referred to as a marriage is the salvation previously announced.

5. How does God's restoration take place? (See Isaiah 53.)

God's restoration takes place in the fulfillment of Isaiah 53 when Yahweh, the Suffering Servant, saves us by His sacrificial suffering and death.

6. **How has the Messiah dressed His Bride in righteousness?**

   Jesus took the filthy rags of our sins and has dressed us in the righteousness He earned by His perfect obedience to the Law.

   ___

   ___

   ___

   ___

7. **How are the comparisons in this text helpful in understanding our relationship with God?**

   The marriage covenant of salvation is a covenant of actions by God and reception, then response, by God's people. These words are helpful in themselves and will be helpful when we get to the discussion about Ephesians 5.

   ___

   ___

   ___

8. **What do righteousness and salvation have to do with the changes and blessings that are described in Isaiah 62:2–12?**

   Righteousness and salvation bring about the changes and blessings that are described in Isaiah 62:2–12. They are the result of God's action toward us in the marriage covenant of salvation.

   ___

   ___

9. **Why were the name changes necessary?**

The name changes are a result of God's action in the marriage covenant of salvation. God changes His Bride. The names change because the people are changed.

10. **What did God do to make those new names true for sinners like us?**

God's grace to us in Christ makes this true.

11. **What do the texts from this lesson have in common?**

They all speak of the marriage covenant of salvation that God has made with Israel, His church.

12. How are the texts from this lesson different?

They all bring a different perspective to the marriage covenant. Have participants point out some of the differences (marriage ceremony; identification of Yahweh, the Creator and Redeemer, as the husband; clothing of the Bride; the changes the marriage covenant makes).

____

____

____

____

____

13. After working through this lesson, what have you learned about the marriage covenant of salvation? How would you apply these truths in marriage?

Ask participants what they have learned.

____

____

____

____

LEADER GUIDE

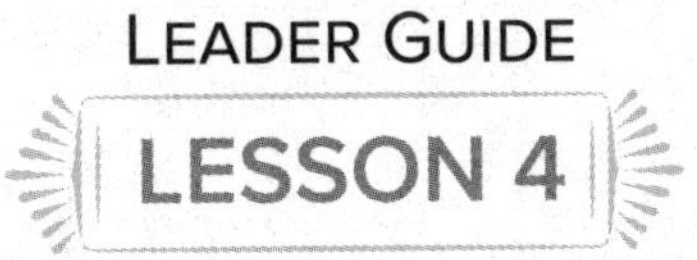

GOD'S RESPONSE TO ISRAEL'S SINFULNESS

OPENING NOTE: With the possible exception of Jeremiah 31, these texts are likely not familiar to your group. The language in these texts is harsh. Let these texts sink in, then allow time to process them in discussion. The serious nature of sin can, at times, be lost in the careful language we employ in the twenty-first century. Such harsh condemnation makes the grace all the more wondrous.

1. **In what sense was Israel's idolatry an act of spiritual adultery against God?**

   In Jeremiah 2–3, God's Bride had relations with other gods. In the context of the marriage covenant of salvation, such idolatry is adultery.

   ____

   ____

   ____

   ____

2. **What does God speaking about being Israel's Husband have to do with the new covenant?**

His status as Husband comes to fullness in the new covenant fulfilled in the coming Messiah: Jesus.

____

____

____

____

3. **How is this true of the history of God and His people?**

God set His people apart by establishing them from nothing in Abraham. Then He brought them out of bondage in Egypt and made them His own. They continually complained about Him and worshiped other gods. His condemnation was harsh, but He remained true to His promises. He would restore them forever when He sent Jesus as their Savior.

____

____

____

____

4. **How do these texts speak to the issue of how these sexual sins help us understand the severity of our sins against God?**

Their idolatry is portrayed as whoredom (sexual sin). Sexual sins, which are so common in our society, have no place in Christianity. There must always be a call to repentance followed by forgiveness and restoration in God's grace. We have all been touched by the hurt and separation so often caused by sexual sins. We always seek restoration through forgiveness. It may take time for repentance to come, and sometimes it may never come at all. We persist in our love for those in error, part of which is continual prayer and work toward resolution.

____

____

____

____

5. **How does the harsh tone in this text add to the discussion of idolatry and sexual sins then and now?**

   Sexual sin is spoken of in Scripture with great vitriol, probably because of the tie between faithfulness in marriage and God's faithfulness in His covenant with us. Such harsh language speaks to the seriousness of our sins, the damnation they deserve, and the vital importance of the subject of salvation.

____

____

____

____

6. **How is Hosea's prophetic ministry different from most other prophets?**

In this text, the prophet is called to marry a prostitute, not just to expose the harlotry of Israel with words. The life of the prophet becomes a visual message to Israel.

7. Why does God frequently change the names He gives His people in this section of Scripture?

As in Isaiah 62, the name changes are a result of the grace of God in bringing His people back into the marriage covenant of salvation. Israel is restored, and her children become part of the change.

8. How, and when, does this happen in a Christian's life?

All this will happen when the Messiah comes to fulfill the marriage covenant of salvation.

9. **What do these texts say about idolatry?**

   They say it is unfaithfulness to God and is the ultimate abomination that separates us from Him.

   ____

   ____

   ____

   ____

10. **What do these texts say about God's faithfulness to us and our faithfulness to Him?**

    God is faithful to us regardless of whether we are faithful to Him. He continued His promised covenant of salvation with Israel despite her adulterous idolatry.

    ____

    ____

    ____

    ____

11. **What might similar prophets say about idolatry and faithfulness in the church now?**

God has kept His promise and sent Jesus to bring about the marriage covenant of salvation forever. Unfaithfulness comes in many forms in the church today (false teaching, accommodating cultural views, relative truth, and so on) and is to be just as forcefully condemned as it was in Israel. God will remain faithful to His promises. Repentance is constantly needed. Forgiveness and restoration are constantly given. Grace is greater than our feeble practice.

____

____

____

____

12. What do these texts say about adultery? How do we apply that to the world we live in today, especially within the institution of marriage?

Adultery, along with all other sexual sins, is an abomination to God. That is true in both the Old and New Testaments. We cannot countenance sexual sins within the church. Repentance is essential so that forgiveness may restore sinners.

____

____

____

____

LEADER GUIDE

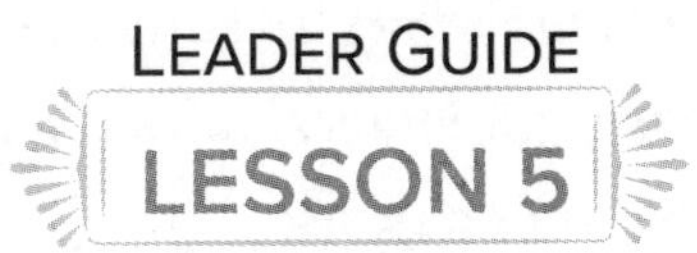

THE SONG OF SOLOMON

The Ephesians 5 of the Old Testament

OPENING NOTE: Many Christians have never read the Song of Solomon. Those who have are at best confused and at worst befuddled by what they read. Most simply move on and don't return without contemplating the purpose and message of the Song of Solomon. Assume nothing about those in your group regarding their understanding of the Song of Solomon. Take the time to lead participants through this Word of God, seeing it through the lens of salvation.

1. **Based on what we have read, how does the marriage covenant of salvation raise Christian marriage to a higher calling?**

   Marriage is not just the joining of two into one. It is also a reflection of the marriage covenant between God and His people. That marriage covenant is the covenant of salvation. As we will discuss further in Lesson 8, Christian marriage is a confession of our faith in what Jesus has done for us by saving us and of how we respond to His gracious gift.

2. **What do these words mean in relation to the discussion of faithfulness?**

   Faithfulness begins with chastity before marriage. These words call us away from the simple urges we experience as males and females to the realization that we are part of something far more important than just our feelings and urges. Our faithfulness before marriage is primarily faithfulness to God and secondarily to the person He may give us as a spouse.

   ____

   ____

   ____

   ____

3. **What do these garden references mean in relation to our discussion of the Song of Solomon?**

   These references lead us to the Garden of Eden and the one-flesh unity of a man and a woman in marriage. God took the rib from Adam and made Eve. He then united them in the one-flesh relationship of marriage. The garden images in the Song of Solomon are also a foreshadowing of the reality in which we live—the uniting of God and the church in the death and resurrection of Jesus.

   ____

   ____

   ____

   ____

4. **How can this be reflected by Christian men and women before and during marriage?**

   Men can reflect Jesus by leading in love. A man should guard his own and his spouse's virginity before marriage by having honorable conduct and cherishing her in marriage with complete fidelity. A woman should receive her husband's love and respect before marriage, not seeking to seduce; then she should receive her husband's love and faithfulness in marriage and respond in love and faithfulness.

   ____

   ____

   ____

   ____

5. **What is the difference between yearning or attraction and lust?**

   To desire to marry at some point and live in intimate expression of your unity is one thing. To selfishly and obsessively want satisfaction of fleshly desires in contradiction of God's will is lust, thus sin.

   ____

   ____

   ____

   ____

6. **Why does God forbid sexual intercourse apart from marriage? (See Genesis 2:18–24; Matthew 19:1–6.)**

   Sexual intercourse is the expression of the one-flesh unity God has made by joining a man and woman in marriage. Participation in intercourse apart from that marriage is a denial of the faithfulness of God in the marriage covenant of salvation.

   ____

   ____

   ____

   ____

7. **How does the part of the Song of Solomon before Solomon and his wife's wedding remind us of the Old Testament times, the present times, or both?**

   God continually came to Israel in love, promising her a covenant relationship that would be fulfilled in His coming as the Messiah. We live in the New Testament era awaiting Jesus' return to bring us to paradise with Him forever.

   ____

   ____

   ____

   ____

8. **How does Solomon's wedding remind us of the coming of Christ in the New Testament or His return?**

   God fulfilled His promise, making His people His Bride when He bore the filthy rags of our sins and dressed us in His righteousness.

   ____

   ____

   ____

   ____

9. **How does the period after Solomon's wedding remind us of today or of heaven?**

   We live in a time when we continually yearn for Jesus' presence and live in that presence and His grace until He returns to give us the fulfillment in heaven.

   ____

   ____

   ____

   ____

10. What does the Song of Solomon teach us about our relationship to God?

Our relationship to God as the church is described in Scripture as a marriage covenant. He makes His covenant with us by delivering His gifts of grace. He makes us His own by His sacrificial love for us. We receive His love and faithfulness and respond with love and faithfulness to Him.

____

____

____

____

11. How do those lessons apply to your marriage?

A husband is called to deliver God's gifts (love and faithfulness) to his wife by following God's example. A wife receives that love and faithfulness and shows it to her husband.

____

____

____

____

12. What can people who are dating or preparing for marriage learn from the Song of Solomon?

There is a godly way to search for and find a spouse. Solomon and his bride are good examples for us. Our calling includes sexual faithfulness before marriage by heeding the words of the Song of Solomon: "I adjure you . . . that you not stir up or awaken love until it pleases" (2:7; 3:5; 8:4). That time is in marriage when it pleases God.

Have participants consider how these possible aspects of a date mirror God's love for us.

- He comes to the door to get her for the date because Christ came for us, while she receives him joyfully as the church receives Christ.

____

____

____

____

____

- He opens the door for her because Jesus opens the door to God's grace and glory. She thankfully goes in as the church enters into the blessings God has prepared.

____

____

____

____

____

- He does the seemingly small thing of paying for the meal in recognition and thanks for the wondrous things Christ did for the church, which he is part of. She expresses her thanks for the blessings as the church does in liturgy and hymns.

____

____

____

____

- He shows her love, honor, and respect by not asking her to compromise the gift of her sexuality. She honors him by her faithfulness to their premarital calling.

____

____

____

____

- He brings her home safely as Christ delivers us safely to heaven. She rejoices in what she has received, just as the church rejoices in what Christ has done and does.

____

____

All of these are suggestions for possibly raising dating to something higher. These should not be considered rules or necessary guidelines. Reflecting the marriage covenant of salvation in and out of marriage should be a joyous calling, not a yoke of burden.

____

____

____

____

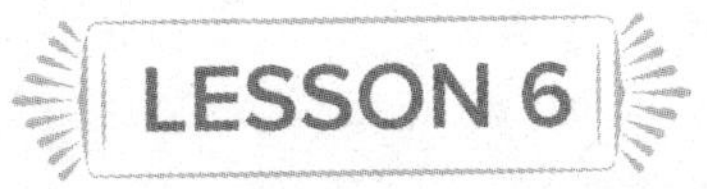

MARRIAGE COVENANT LANGUAGE IN THE GOSPELS

OPENING NOTE: We will now discuss the actual ministry of Jesus revealed in the four Gospels. This will be a discussion of texts that refer or allude to the Old Testament texts previously studied. In many cases, Jesus Himself referred to the Old Testament language. Previously, we discussed what would be. This discussion will be about how those texts are fulfilled in Jesus.

1. **Is there any question that Jesus is the Bridegroom in this parable? Why or why not?**

   The context of these verses leaves no doubt that Jesus is the Bridegroom, thus the fulfillment of the Old Testament marriage covenant of salvation.

   ____

   ____

   ____

   ____

2. **Who are the "wedding guests"?**

   As Jesus is the Bridegroom, His disciples are the friends of the Bridegroom.

   ____

   ____

   ____

   ____

3. **How are these words similar to those in the Old Testament?**

   "Adulterous," in particular, reminds us of the language of Jeremiah, Ezekiel, and Hosea. The idolatry of Israel is called adultery in the Old Testament texts.

   ____

   ____

   ____

   ____

4. **How did the people Jesus condemned commit adultery or idolatry?**

   The adulterous idolatry of those in Jesus' day was their rejection of Yahweh as He revealed Himself in the Old Testament, exchanging the God of grace for an idol of Law. Because they did not truly know the God they claimed to serve, they rejected Him when He became incarnate to save them.

   ____

5. **What is the common occasion in these two texts?**

   Both parables depict a wedding.

6. **What does it mean to be locked out of this event?**

   To be locked out of this event is to be excluded from God's kingdom. To be locked out is to be excluded from the marriage covenant of salvation, which means eternal destruction.

7. **When did Jesus provide the feast?**

   The texts describing the marriage covenant of salvation were fulfilled when God restored His Bride to Himself forever. That is the fulfillment of the covenant of salvation in the death and resurrection of Jesus.

8. **How did He accomplish this?**

He accomplished this by saving us in the fulfillment of God's eternal plan. This took place when Jesus took our sins on Himself, dying on the cross for our sins and rising to assure us of His promises, especially resurrection to eternal life.

9. **What did John the Baptist prepare the people for?**

John prepared the people for the coming of the Messiah. He pointed out the mission of Jesus in John 1:29: "Behold, the Lamb of God, who takes away the sin of the world!"

10. What does John the Baptist preparing people have to do with the marriage covenant of salvation?

In ancient weddings, the best man was sent out into the town at sundown to announce the coming of the bridegroom. John the Baptist fulfilled that task by identifying himself as the best man, thus identifying Jesus as the Bridegroom.

____

____

____

____

11. How do these texts show the marriage covenant of salvation fulfilled in Jesus?

All of them deal with some aspect of the marriage covenant. Jesus is the Bridegroom in all of them. He is the promised Bridegroom. Salvation has been accomplished through Him.

____

____

____

____

12. What facets of ancient marriage customs do we see in these texts?

We see the announcement by the best man and by the servants of the king (Matthew 22:1–4). We also see the preparation and anticipation by the bride and her attendants (Matthew 25). We also see the feast in parable and reality (Matthew 22:1–4; John 2:1–12).

____

____

13. How does Jesus affirming that He is the Bridegroom help us understand the Old Testament marriage texts?

In the more positive Old Testament texts (e.g., Isaiah 54; 61; 62), the marriage covenant is tied to the saving work of the Suffering Servant (Isaiah 53). In the primarily negative texts (e.g., Ezekiel 16; 23; Hosea 1–14), God promises to restore unfaithful Israel through the promised Savior. Jesus fulfills them all.

____

____

____

____

LEADER GUIDE

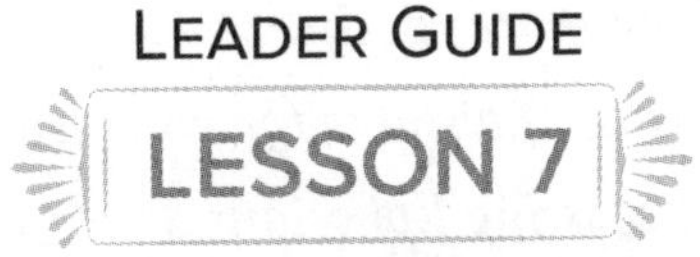

MARRIAGE COVENANT LANGUAGE IN THE EPISTLES AND REVELATION

OPENING NOTE: This lesson is a discussion of the Epistles, except Ephesians 5 (which will be discussed in Lesson 8). Some are obvious references to the marriage covenant of salvation in the Old Testament. Others are less obvious.

1. **What is the dying and new marriage in this text?**

   Paul is referring to the dying to sin and rising again to new life that he explained in Romans 6.

   ____

   ____

   ____

   ____

2. **How do these words help you understand roles within marriage? What questions do they raise?**

   Had the saints in Colossae heard Paul's letter to the Ephesians? We don't know if they did or not. If not, these words provided simple instructions for them to follow. If they did, the content served as a reminder of the more specific teaching of Ephesians 5. These words likely will raise questions for your learners that should be addressed when discussing Ephesians 5.

   ____

   ____

   ____

   ____

3. **What defiles the marriage bed?**

   Sexual sins of any kind defile, as had been implicit in the Song of Solomon, where we are told not to stir up the flame of love until marriage.

   ____

   ____

   ____

   ____

4. **Why do males have greater accountability in the marriage covenant?**

Adam is held accountable for his sin in Genesis 3. Christ bore the ultimate accountability for our sins on the cross, fulfilling the marriage covenant of salvation. A husband reflects this accountability by showing love for his wife.

5. **How is this language like that of the Old Testament prophets?**

   The negatives listed have very similar language. You may want to take participants back to Ezekiel 16; 23; and Hosea 1.

6. **What false teachings threaten the church today?**

   Let participants list false religions (Islam, Hinduism, Mormonism, and so on) and secular beliefs (Darwinism, Marxism, Freudianism, and so on).

7. **What is the marriage feast of the Lamb?**

   The marriage feast of the Lamb is the celebration of the marriage covenant of salvation that is going on in heaven.

8. **How is the new Jerusalem the Bride of Christ?**

   She is the people of God located in heaven.

9. **What is her adornment?**

   She has been dressed in Jesus' righteousness, similar to the language of Isaiah 61; 62.

10. What connection do these texts have with the Old Testament covenant of salvation?

Do a quick review of the references listed in this study.

11. How are the actions of God's people a reflection of that covenant?

The actions of God's people in marriage are a calling to reflect this covenant. This will be discussed in greater detail in Lesson 8.

LEADER GUIDE

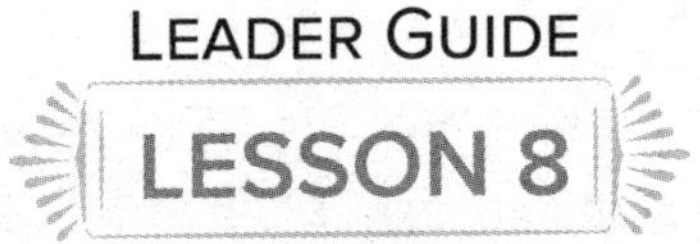

EPHESIANS 5

The Song of Solomon of the New Testament

OPENING NOTE: This text is where the teaching of the marriage covenant of salvation comes together. The Old Testament marriage covenant is identified as the Gospel marriage between Christ and His church. A husband and wife are called to reflect that in their love for each other. Take the time to let participants discuss the teaching of Scripture in this lesson.

1. **What does a Christian's participation in sexual sins wrongly imply about God and His covenant with us?**

   Sexual sins are the antithesis of the marriage covenant of salvation. Christians confess their faith by the way they reflect Him in their love. All sins are a contrary confession of actions. Sexual sins are a particular contrary confession about God's marriage covenant with us.

   ____

   ____

2. **In Paul's comparison of Christ and the church to a husband and wife, how does Paul show that a marriage between a man and a woman reflects the relationship between Christ and the church?**

   Paul compares Christ and the church to the love and subjection a husband and wife have and show for each other. (Reread Ephesians 5:22–30 and emphasize the repeated use of the word as *to show the relationship between a Christian marriage and Christ's love for the church). Paul affirms this in verses 32–33. The language of the marriage covenant of salvation is biblical imagery, but Jesus truly laid down His life for the church, and the church truly receives what He did and responds in prayer, praise, and loving service to others. Jesus as our Savior is not biblical imagery. The church as the redeemed is not imagery. The imagery of this true relationship is the mystery Paul speaks of. The image speaks to the greatest reality of all.*

   ___

   ___

   ___

   ___

3. **What is the church's response to the loving sacrifice Jesus made for us? What does that look like in congregational life?**

The church receives the sacrifice of Jesus and responds in joy with prayer, praise, and confession of faith. That includes worship and the life of the church. The church, in joy for what Christ has done, is the vessel through which the children of God are born in Baptism and conversion and through which God's children are nurtured through Word and Sacrament.

---

4. **In this calling, what is the motivation for your conduct as a husband or wife?**

   We are motivated by the love we have received from Christ. We must be careful not to make our part simply a burden of Law. Reflecting Christ is not a new and unattainable requirement for husbands, but He is a wondrous example husbands should respond to with joy and faith. The church is not some idealistic, unreachable standard of conduct, but it is an example of how to receive God's love and respond in joy.

---

5. **What do these relationships look like in your home?**

   They look like the love of Jesus voluntarily given by each to the other. They are selfless acts done simply because you love your spouse. Forgiveness is given and received because of the forgiveness of Christ. Having learned love at the cross, we show it.

   ____

   ____

   ____

   ____

6. **Why is it important for a man to love his wife and for a woman to respect her husband?**

   God knows those He has created. While both gifts are needed from each other, women most need the security that comes from being completely loved. Men most need the respect that affirms their self-sacrifice.

   ____

   ____

   ____

   ____

APPENDIX

ANCIENT JEWISH WEDDINGS

The following is a list of the Jewish marriage customs in biblical times. It will help us better understand aspects of the marriage analogy that are different compared to our dating, engagement, and wedding practices. We don't know how these customs came to be. Did they arise from the cultural understanding of the biblical texts we have studied? We do know that some of these texts were understood as being about God's relationship to Israel. The Jewish Mishnah (Jacob Neusner, *The Mishnah: A New Translation* [Yale University Press, 1988], 316) references specific events in the Old Testament (the giving of the Torah; the building of the temple) as being portrayed in the words of the Song of Solomon. The practices listed below are similar to the practices followed in Jewish weddings today. This is an outline of the customs and biblical texts that appear to reference the following customs.

BETROTHAL (PAYING THE BRIDE PRICE)

- The groom would approach the father in person or through an intermediary.
- The father would give permission, and the two would be betrothed, creating a binding agreement.
- The groom would pay a bride price as a guarantee of his promise.
- Bible references:

  Song of Solomon 2

Isaiah 61:8–11

Ezekiel 16:1–14

Matthew 1:18–25

THE BUILDING OF THE BRIDAL CHAMBER, ASSEMBLING OF THE DOWRY

- The groom would build the bridal chamber onto his father's house.
- The bride would assemble her dowry of things she would bring to her marriage.
- Bible references:

  Song of Solomon 3:1–5

  John 14:2–3

THE GATHERING OF THE MAIDENS

- There was not a set date for the wedding. The wedding took place when the groom was ready.
- The day of the wedding was always the middle day of the week (our Wednesday).
- When it appeared the wedding may be near, the bride's friends would gather at her home on Tuesday afternoon to be ready for the wedding.
- Bible references:

  Song of Solomon 1

  Matthew 25:1–13

  Revelation 19:6–8

  Revelation 21:2

THE SENDING OF THE BEST MAN

- On the day of the wedding (sometime after sunset), the groom would send out his friend (the best man), who would cry out that the bridegroom was coming.
- The maids would quickly finish preparing the bride for the groom, who could arrive at any time.
- The people of the town would prepare to attend the wedding and the very lengthy feast.
- Bible references:

  Malachi 3:1

  John 3:22–30

THE COMING OF THE BRIDEGROOM

- The groom and his friends would take the bride to the courtyard of his father's house, where the people were gathered for the wedding.
- Bible references:

  Psalm 45

  Song of Solomon 3:6–11

  Matthew 25:1–13

THE WEDDING

- The couple wed under a canopy in the courtyard. The wedding took place under the stars in remembrance of God's promise to Abraham in Genesis 22:17.

- The groom would promise his covenant of faithfulness, after which he would drink wine from a cup and smash it, signifying that the wedding was complete.
- Bible references:

  Psalm 45

  Song of Solomon 4:1–16

  Isaiah 62:1–5

THE WEDDING FEAST

- The groom would take the bride into the wedding chamber to consummate the marriage.
- The feast lasted until the food and wine were gone (usually about a week).
- For most of the feast, the bride remained in the bridal chamber. The groom would bring her the feast while the others celebrated outside.
- Near the end of the feast, the bride and groom would join the feast together.
- Bible references:

  Matthew 22:1–14

  John 2:1–11

  Revelation 19:9–10